CONTENTS

About the author

Robin Capon is a freelance writer and artist. He is the author of 12 books on art and craft techniques and writes regularly for *The Artist* and *Leisure Painter* magazines. His drawings and paintings are sold through various provincial exhibitions and galleries.

Formerly a teacher of some considerable experience, he now runs a number of holiday painting courses in North Devon, works as an examination moderator for the Southern Examining Group and is an A-level course tutor for the National Extension College.

—— INTRODUCTION ——

In essence, most drawings are simply a collection of marks on a sheet of paper. To make those marks all you need to be able to do is to look, think and hold a pencil – so it's probable that you can already draw to some extent! Of course, some people can draw much better than others. This may be because they have greater innate skill, or, more likely, because they have had more practice and have been better taught.

People draw for different reasons. Some drawings need to be accurate and realistic, while others can be a free and uninhibited expression of your feelings. Whatever the reason for drawing, you will always find it rewarding and enjoyable.

Throughout this book there are examples of drawings by famous artists. If you study the art and artefacts of any period of history you will see that people have always wanted to draw. It is a natural form of self-expression and a way of showing what we think and feel about things. What is more, drawing is not restricted by the frontiers of language. Illustration **1**, a drawing by the Dutch artist Van Gogh, is full of feeling and personality: we can understand and react to the drawing whatever our language.

We are all born with an ability to draw; our first marks are usually in the form of drawing rather than writing. Because we can all draw, given some time, practice and perseverence, we can improve the way we see and express our ideas through this versatile medium. Ideally, drawing is a continuous, developing activity. So, if you haven't drawn for a number of

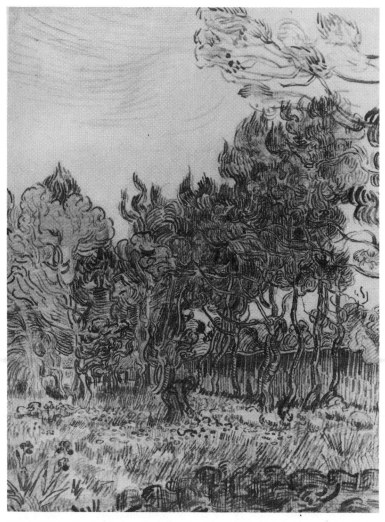

Illustration 1 *A Garden at St Remy* by Vincent Van Gogh. Pen and ink. Tate Gallery, London

years you are bound to have lost some skill and confidence. And even if you draw regularly, there are always fresh ideas to explore and new media to try out. But it is never too late to start drawing or to improve your technique.

To draw successfully doesn't just depend on competent technique. Drawing involves looking and understanding, selecting and interpreting, as well as using imagination and employing various procedures and methods. It is a demanding activity, for you need to look, think and draw almost simultaneously. More than anything else it needs enthusiasm and the will to try out a variety of methods, and to have another go when things do not quite work. The more you draw, the more you will discover about yourself and which techniques and ideas you wish to develop further.

There is no such thing as a 'proper' way to draw. Like handwriting, drawing is a personal form of communicating. This does not mean that you cannot learn from looking at other drawings or by practising exercises and techniques. But as your work develops, so all of this experience will be assimilated into your individual way of drawing.

You will see that this book is divided into two parts. The first part, 'Materials and Methods', will get you thinking about why we draw, the variety of materials that can be used, and the basic techniques. You will discover that an important aspect of learning to draw is learning to see, understand and visually analyse things. From this foundation of information, activities and experience, you will be able to progress to part two, 'Developing Ideas', in which you can tackle the more challenging questions of composition and working through different stages, as well as find many ideas to help you develop your own style of drawing.

Using this well-structured approach, you should be able to build on information, examples, suggestions and topics to improve your drawing skills, whatever your ability. The best way to learn to draw is to have a go for yourself, so throughout the book you will be encouraged to try out the ideas and techniques and set up your own assignments and exercises along the lines of the general projects for each section.

One of the great fascinations of drawing is the variety of possible approaches and interpretations. As you gain experience, don't be afraid to let your own ideas and personality influence your work, and, above all, enjoy yourself!

1
——————— WHAT IS ———————
DRAWING?

As you work through this book you will see that a drawing can be just a few simple lines or, contrastingly, a highly detailed study. You might choose to draw freely with a brush dipped in ink, or work intricately with a sharp HB pencil. Your drawing can be perceived as a starting point or as the finished product. Drawings can be informative, expressive and decorative, just as they can be funny or serious, therapeutic or intellectual. There are cartoons and illustrations, plans and diagrams, roughs and sketches, and details and studies. A drawing can be scratched in the sand or printed from a computer – the scope is vast.

Defining drawing is no easy task. Certainly, drawing involves making strokes or marks on any suitable surface to communicate or suggest ideas and information. It is, therefore, a means of expression and a method of contact between the artist and other people. But, contrary to the definition in many dictionaries, drawing is not confined to lines and monochrome. There are many colour drawing techniques today, as demonstrated in the two colour sections of this book. In addition, some drawing methods rely on washes or broad areas and applications of tone, rather than lines. And, like painting, a drawing can be made with a brush. Often, the initial stages of a painting are in fact drawing, this evolving into the reliance on colour and form and the bolder use of brush and paint which marks a painting. Consequently, boundaries between drawing and painting remain imprecise.

In general terms, however, most drawings use line as the principle technique and are made in black and white. Usually the method is to press a soft substance, like pencil or charcoal, on to a harder, receptive surface, like paper, to create a series of marks. Equally, drawings can be made by an intaglio or impressed process, as well as by carving, indenting, spraying and other methods.

When we look at things we see them as form and colour, not in terms of lines. In creating a drawing we are, therefore, frequently assessing what we see and transcribing this image into a series of lines, dashes and dots. Although this process can reach heights of great sophistication, conveying likeness and realism, theoretically all drawings must simplify, abstract and interpret what is actually seen.

Vital marks

Many people think of good drawing in terms of accuracy and realism. Presumably these are the qualities they are striving for in their wish to improve their drawing skills. Others concentrate on techniques and the means to express. Of course, we can all draw to some extent and, ironically, the ultimate in criticism is 'anyone can make a few marks on a bit of paper'! The trouble is that as we grow up we develop preconceptions and inhibitions which undermine our confidence to draw freely.

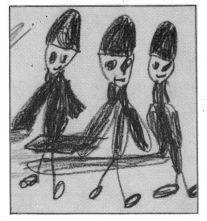

Illustration   **2**   *Policemen* A lively, spontaneous drawing in wax crayon by a four year old

Look at illustration **2**. How most of us will envy the sheer joy and uninhibited approach of this young artist! There is nothing rubbed out, fussed over, cluttered or overworked here. The drawings of young children are characterised by clear and immediate statements about what is felt. They are acts of communication which are often easier and more successfully made than verbal expression. The marks are vital and telling. What a pity that we have to grow up.

The more you draw the more you will understand that successful drawings depend on doing just the right amount of work. A good drawing conveys the artist's message with some impact yet at the same time often leaves something to the imagination of the viewer. Simple drawings are frequently very powerful. Look at the splendid Guercino nude (illustration **148**, page 143), for example. This succeeds in implying a good deal which isn't actually drawn, combining this with lines of great spontaneity and energy. Learning to simplify is a key element in the process of learning to draw.

But this isn't to say that all subjects must be reduced to a few lines. Often, there are very good reasons to render detail, textures and highly accurate shapes. Why you choose to draw something and how you choose to interpret it are obviously important factors in determining the sort of drawing you make. It may well be that to express what you see as the essential characteristics of your subject you need to use a variety of techniques and go into a fair amount of detail. However, whether you use a few lines or many hundreds, everything should count and contribute towards the end result. Each mark should be vital.

The language of drawing

There is a well-known Chinese saying that 'a picture is worth a thousand words'. In illustration **3** it would take several highly descriptive paragraphs accurately to relate the detail and characteristics of this old barn and its rural surrounds. Yet you can scan a drawing in a few seconds and the message is conveyed almost immediately and possibly with more impact and information. Additionally, of course, the language of drawing is international and, as long as you can see, will mean something to you whatever your culture and background.

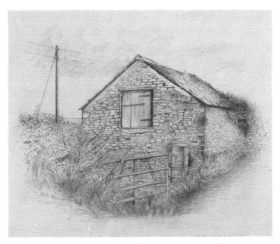

Illustration   3   Drawing to convey detail and description. Pencil

The fact that we can read a drawing quite quickly need not lessen its lasting value. The best drawings never tire in their appeal and, like any good work of art, we will always find them interesting and stimulating to look at, noticing fresh things to understand and appreciate.

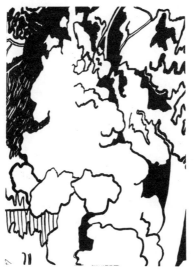

Illustration   4   Expression: a personal response to a subject. Brush and ink

If there is a general language of drawing there are obviously many subtle variations of that language from artist to artist. Illustration **4**, for example, is much more expressive and subjective than the pencil studies in illustrations **3** and **5**. If we have an affinity towards certain artists or particular drawings it is because we more clearly understand the language. And, to take this one stage further, each artist can employ variations of his or her drawing language according to the aims of the drawing. Working roughs are made to clarify ideas, sketchbook studies to collect information, and the final drawing to resolve our thoughts into a visual statement. Each of these stages of working requires a different sort of approach and emphasis.

—————— Types of drawing ——————

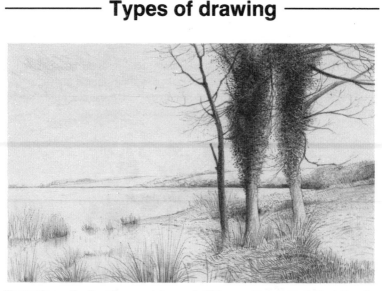

Illustration   5   Drawings can inform yet still be sensitive and individual. Pencil

Mostly we draw to inform or to express. If we want to show what something looks like we are usually 'objective' and representational in our approach; if we wish to show what we feel about something, then we are more likely to be 'subjective' and expressive. This is classifying drawing into very broad types, of course. Drawings such as those in illustrations **5** and **6** are representational and informative yet not entirely objective, for

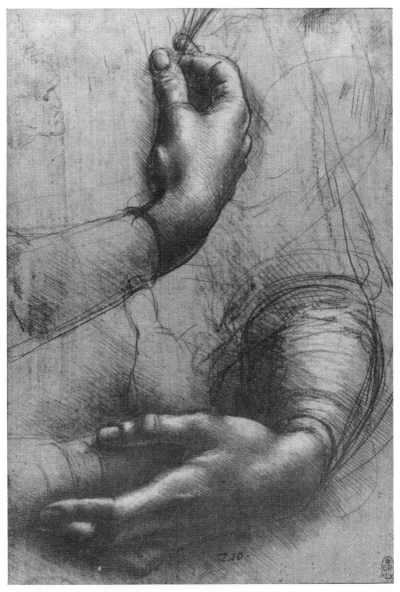

Illustration 6 *Study of Hands* by Leonardo da Vinci. Chalk. Windsor Castle, Royal Library, © Her Majesty the Queen

they are drawn with some feeling. Similarly, a subjective drawing like the Van Gogh *Garden at St. Remy* (illustration **1**) is full of feeling while still managing to inform.

Drawings which inform normally result from straightforward observation and enquiry. Such drawings aim to create records of fact. This process can be carried further into detailed analysis: there is something of this in the Leonardo *Hands* (illustration **6**). Where the artist's personal response to the subject dominates, emotion is likely to replace quiet observation and results might vary from something which is freely and passionately drawn, to works which are non-objective or completely abstract in concept.

Linked to our response to the subject and our aims and objectives for undertaking the drawing is the method best suited fully to realise the idea. Vital to the success of any drawing is the medium we choose and the consequent range of techniques. So, as well as being objective or subjective, representational or expressive, analytical or stylised, decorative or abstract, drawings can also be classified by medium and method: pencil, pen and ink, charcoal, mixed media, and so on. There are also line drawings, tonal drawings, line and wash, and a range of other techniques. And, as previously mentioned, drawing types may be thumbnail sketches, diagrammatic summaries, roughs, cartoons, details, underdrawing for painting, research studies and large-scale completed works.

Think of your drawings in terms of:

- approach – objective or subjective
- method – pencil, line and wash, etc.
- outcome – sketch, study, highly resolved drawing, etc.

The next two chapters of this book, 'Choosing Your Materials' and 'Looking, Seeing and Interpreting', will help you understand more about the range of available materials and the different ways of looking and selecting.

Why do we draw?

From cave art to computers, people have always felt the need to draw. It is a natural form of expression and communication. We draw out of curiosity and interest, to help us understand things, solve problems, get information or resolve ideas. Ideally we draw because there is an urge, an inspiration, a desire to commit ideas to paper. It is a great way of showing what we think and feel about things.

Drawing isn't always easy: it can be very demanding and difficult. But it should always be rewarding. Already you will have an indication of the exciting scope of drawing. Whatever philosophy you evolve towards the subject you will find that there are plenty of ideas and techniques to choose from – something for everyone. And the more involved you become with drawing, the more you practise, the greater will be your enjoyment. You will soon discover that tremendous sense of achievement and satisfaction when a drawing is completed and it exactly states your intentions.

———————— What can we use? ————————

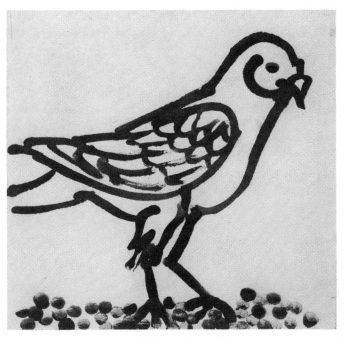

Illustration   7 Be adventurous and experiment! This drawing was made with a finger dipped in some black poster paint

Everyone doodles occasionally, probably on the telephone pad while waiting for an answer or half-listening to someone. It is obvious that most drawings can be done very simply. Unlike many other forms of art, they do not need a lot of complicated equipment and expensive materials. Indeed, this is often proven when you are out, see a splendid subject to draw, but do not have any obvious drawing equipment with you. I have made drawings on a brown paper bag, on a blank page at the end of a paperback book, on lined paper . . . even on a car parking voucher!

Most drawings are made with pencil on paper. While this is suitable for many ideas, don't be afraid of being adventurous and of experimenting. The drawing in illustration **7**, for example, was made with a finger dipped in some black poster paint. Playing safe isn't always the best approach and, as has been stressed, you will need to consider which medium and technique will be best for the idea you have in mind. Try to familiarise yourself with as many different drawing materials and methods as possible. Charcoal, pastels, crayons, pens, inks and other materials are introduced in the next chapter, and in 'Learning the basic techniques' (Chapter 4) you will see many ways of using these materials.

Project

Start a drawing scrapbook. Keep in it any postcards and cuttings of famous drawings, subjects which appeal to you and any other visual material which could inspire drawings. Aim for a wide choice of material. In time this will form a very useful reference aid along with your notebooks and sketchbooks.

2
—— CHOOSING ——
YOUR MATERIALS

The first step towards developing your drawing skills is to gain some familiarity and confidence with a wide range of drawing tools and materials. You will soon find that each medium has its particular characteristics and in consequence will help you create certain effects. As you gain experience you will be able to choose the best medium for the type of drawing you want to do, and even combine a variety of different techniques and media.

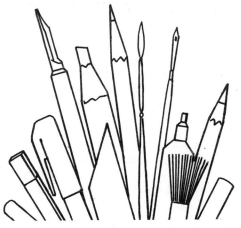

Illustration **8** Collect together a wide range of tools and materials

Read through the whole of this chapter first and then study each drawing medium in more detail. Collect together as many of the tools and materials as you can and test them out by completing the recommended projects at the end. Try colour as well as black and white techniques. Look through the colour sections following pages 48 and 102 to get some ideas.

Pencils

Choose good quality graphite drawing pencils. These are marked to indicate their degree of hardness, usually from 2H to 6B. Very hard pencils, such as 2H, are not normally suitable for general drawing. They cannot be handled with the same sensitivity as softer pencils and tend to indent the paper, thus making it difficult to erase lines which are wrong. Keep to a softer range to begin with: B, 2B, 4B and 6B. Add to these if you feel it is necessary.

One of the first things you will notice is that pencils respond to the pressure you apply. Some people naturally work more confidently and positively than others. Your range of pencils will need to match the way that you work so that you can achieve a good balance of tones and lines from very dark to very light. Also, the response from a 2B pencil, for example, may vary according to the manufacturer. So try out several makes and when you have found a type that handles well, stick to it. You will also notice that the sort of paper you choose will influence the effects you can achieve and the way that pencils and other materials respond.

Supplement your basic drawing pencils with wide carpenters' pencils and graphite sticks for making quick sketches and general tones (light and dark effects). Later, you should try working directly with various types of coloured pencils, including water-soluble pencils. These can be used dry as well as wetted to create various tonal and texture effects. See colour illustration **13**.

At the end of this section you will see that I encourage you to test out all your materials to find out just what variety of lines, dots, dashes, tones and other effects they can give. I hope you will be keen to go further than this and make some small drawings of your own inspired by the accompanying examples. Bear the advice, information and instruction in mind as you draw. But the great thing about drawing is that you learn from experience – so have a go.

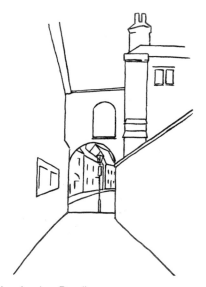

Illustration 9 Line drawing. Pencil

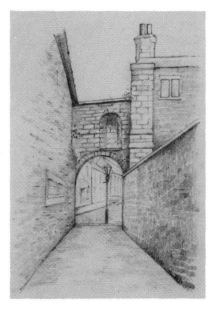

Illustration 10 Tone study. Pencil

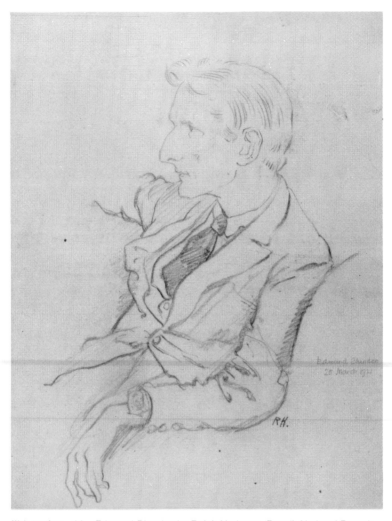

Illustration 11 *Edmund Blunden* by Ralph Hodgson. Pencil. National Portrait Gallery, London

The many pencil drawings in this book prove the range and versatility of this medium. You can see from illustrations **9** to **12** that pencil is just as effective for simple line work as it is for showing detail, tone and texture. Try one or two similar drawings of your own.

—————————— **Charcoal** ——————————

Compressed sticks of willow charcoal are now produced by firing willow rods in a kiln until the wood is carbonized. You can buy boxes of mixed thicknesses, from very thin to thick scene-painters' charcoal. A few sticks are always useful, especially for sketching and loose, large-scale work, as well as for creating greys, diffused shading effects and various textures and dabs of tone in conjunction with other drawing techniques.

Initial experiments with charcoal tend to be rather disappointing, so persevere! Charcoal sticks are brittle, need sensitive and careful handling to create fine lines and controlled work, and can be messy. However, when more positive lines and details are required stick charcoal can be combined with charcoal pencils. These are available in soft, medium and hard qualities and, if used with restrained pressure, will behave just like ordinary pencils.

As an introduction to charcoal, break off a length of about 4cm. Hold this at various angles and apply different pressures to see what variety of lines and tones you can achieve. Try it on smooth as well as heavier quality paper and even coloured paper. Apply it sparingly at first and experiment with smudging it in different ways: with fingers, a cotton bud or a small piece of cloth or paper. You can also use the charcoal on its side for broad tones and general textures. Completed drawings will need fixing in the way described on page 145.

Charcoal is splendid for sketchbook work and getting a quick impression or feeling for the subject. Have a look at illustrations **13** and **14**. Much of the drawing in illustration **14** has been done with a charcoal pencil, using stick charcoal for the general background effects. The large sketch in illustration **13** was done with a single stick of charcoal and shows the immediacy, liveliness and spontaneity of this often underrated medium.

—————————— **Pastels** ——————————

White chalk or pastel is ideal for use in conjunction with charcoal to create highlights and contrasts. Other colours can be purchased individually or in boxes of an assorted range.

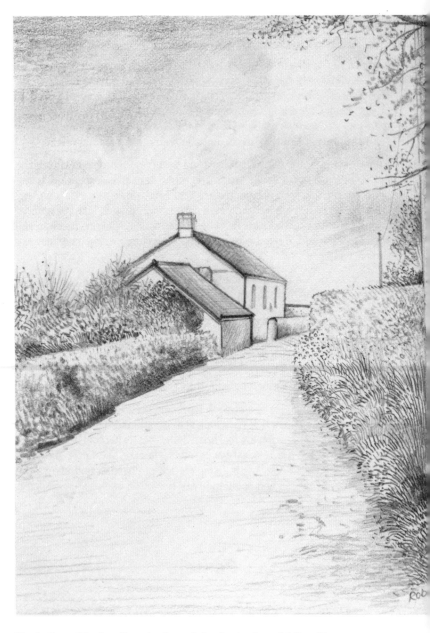

Illustration 12 A well-resolved pencil drawing to show detail and tones

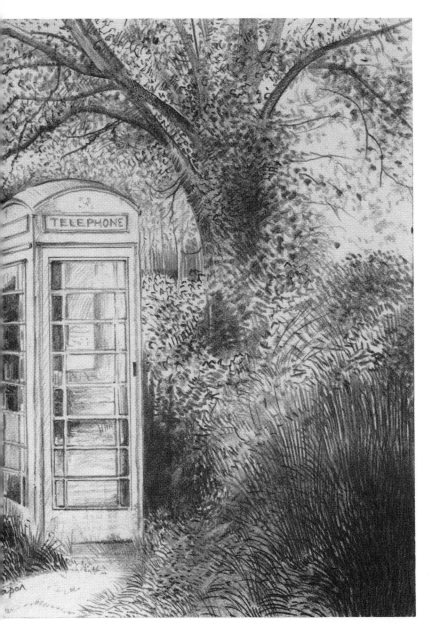

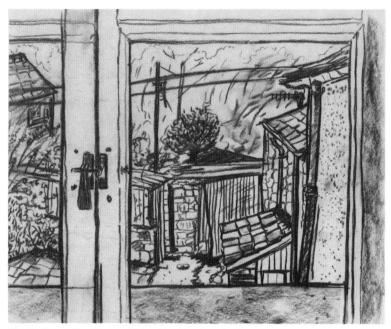

Illustration 13 Charcoal is an ideal medium for lively sketches like this

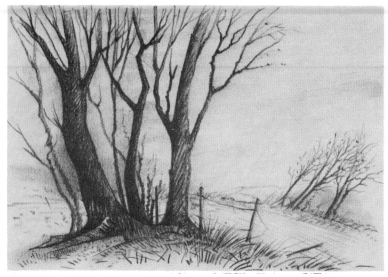

Illustration 14 Landscape study in charcoal pencil

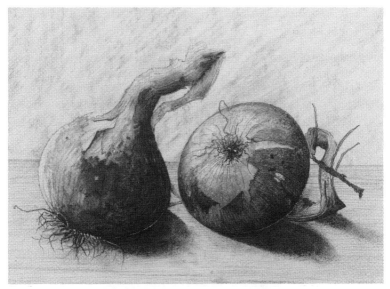

Illustration 15 Using soft pastels and pastel pencils

Learn to distinguish soft pastels, which are like chalks and easy to blend and smudge, from oil pastels, which behave more like wax crayons. On most papers, oil pastels will give rich, solid areas of colour. They are not easy to intermix or erase. Soft pastels, on the other hand, can produce the most delicate of lines as well as subtle chiaroscuro and blended colour effects. Do some experimenting, as recommended for charcoal, so that you get a feel for this medium before attempting some simple drawings.

The general principle with all of these chalk and crayon techniques, indeed with most drawing techniques, is to start with the weak tones and lines and build up the thickness and intensity of the medium gradually. Mix colours either by alternating a line of one colour with another and then blending the two together with a finger or small piece of cloth or paper, or by working one colour over another. Blow away unwanted dust and 'lift' mistakes with a putty rubber.

Illustration **15** shows a number of soft pastel and pastel pencil techniques. Here the main shapes were drawn weakly in pastel pencil. Next the general tones were applied with soft pastel and this was subsequently worked into and over with more deliberate lines and areas of shading using a mixture of pastel pencils and pastel sticks.

Crayons

Under this heading I want you to consider two rather different types of crayon: wax and conté. Wax crayons are often associated with children's drawings and are most suitable as a sketching and 'fun' medium. By contrast, conté crayon drawings seem restricted to a few famous artists, like Seurat.

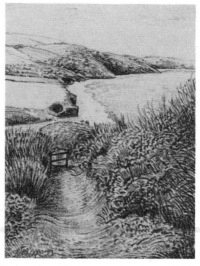

Illustration 16 Wax crayons will give a variety of sensitive line and tone effects

Wax crayons are cheap and a box of assorted colours makes an interesting addition to the range of drawing materials. They can be used for rubbings, quick sketches and a variety of wax resist techniques.

Conté-crayon is a hard, grease-free drawing chalk that is usually applied to heavy quality paper. Like wax crayon, it does not smudge and consequently does not need fixing. It can give lines of great sensitivity as well as dramatic tonal effects. Both types of crayon can be sharpened to create fine lines and, like pastel and charcoal, can be used on their side for general shading.

Illustration **16** was made with a single black wax crayon, by varying the angle and pressure to make lines of different strengths. Wax resist techniques are explained on page 62. See also illustration **145** on page 140.

Pens

These are also inexpensive, so make a collection of as many different kinds as possible. Look out for mapping pens, script pens, technical pens (like Rotring and Staedtler), cartridge pens, ball-point pens, and fibre and felt-tip pens. Dip pens, like mapping and script pens, will need some drawing ink. Additionally, you can experiment by making your own dip pens: sharpen sticks of wood or make a quill.

Each type of pen will give a certain character of line or range of techniques. Dip pens tend to be the more unpredictable since they do not have the controlled flow of ink that a reservoir pen has. Arguably this gives scope for drawings of greater personality, like the reed pen drawings of Van Gogh.

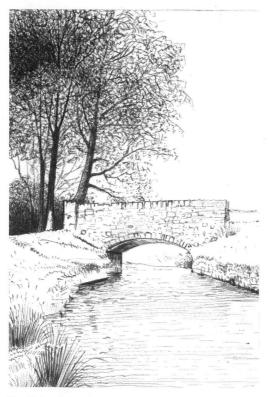

Illustration 17 Ball-point pen

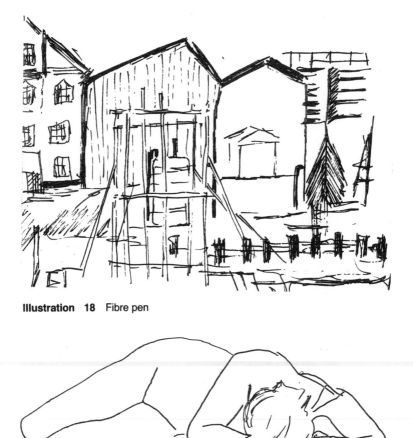

Illustration 18 Fibre pen

Illustration 19 Felt-tip pen

Again, it is a question of trying out each type of pen to see what lines and marks it can make and discover which suits you best. Remember to test each one on some different papers (see page 28).

Many pen techniques are ideal for sketchbook work and quick studies. Look at illustration **17**, for example, which was made with a ballpoint pen, and the two fibre pen drawings in illustrations **18** and **19**. Notice, too, that drawings do not have to be detailed and elaborate to be effective.

Inks

You will see quite a few drawings in this book which have been made with Indian ink, sometimes diluted with water. The ink can be applied with a pen or a brush as specific, direct drawing, or with a brush or sponge for background wash effects. Ink is also used in various spraying, spattering sgraffito and texture techniques, as explained in Chapter 4. Additionally, coloured drawing inks increase the range of possibilities and thin ink washes can be combined with other drawing media and methods.

Start with a small bottle of Indian ink as part of your basic stock of materials. As you gain confidence with this so you can add coloured inks later. Investigate some line drawing techniques using a mapping pen and one or two different brushes. Mix a few drops of ink with a lot of water to make a thin wash. Try applying the wash with a flat watercolour brush or a sponge.

Notice the way that light and dark areas have been created in the ink and brush drawing shown in illustration **20**. The drawing in illustration **21** was made with a mapping pen and Indian ink. The sky effect was made by applying a thin wash of ink to dampened paper.

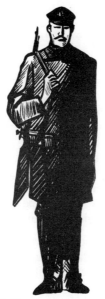

Illustration 20 Dramatic light and dark effects made with a brush and ink

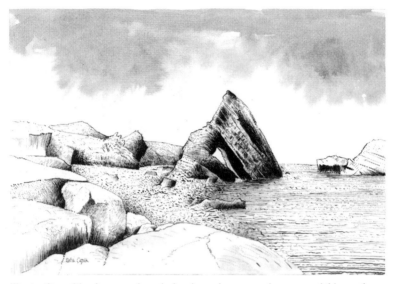

Illustration 21 A pen and wash drawing using a mapping pen and thin washes of very diluted Indian ink

— Other drawing tools and materials —

Drawing tools do not always have to be conventional. When you have mastered some of the basic techniques and started to explore drawings as a personal way of expressing your ideas, you may find that some rather unusual items help in the way you want to work. For example, as well as adapting and modifying tools like brushes and pens, you could try creating texture effects by using part of an old comb or a toothbrush dipped in some ink. You can make unusual drawings by applying a colour wash over lines made with a clear wax candle or by blowing droplets of ink across the paper through a drinking straw. So, don't be afraid to experiment in order to add to your drawing skills; drawing can be fun!

In illustration **22** the lines were drawn with a spent ballpoint pen. Because it had run out of ink the pen simply left indented marks in the paper. When these were shaded over with a soft, 6B pencil they showed up quite clearly. Small blobs of ink will run if the paper is tilted or if they are blown around using a drinking straw blowpipe. This is how the main

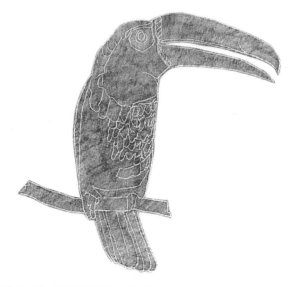

Illustration 22 Impressed line drawing

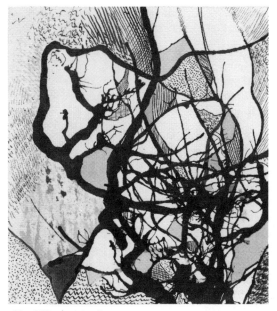

Illustration 23 Different ink effects

part of the drawing in illustration **23** was made. It has created the basis for an abstract drawing in which many of the shapes have been developed with different pen and ink techniques.

Similarly, many people think that drawing is a distinct technique from painting. In fact, the two disciplines often overlap. You can draw with a brush dipped in paint and you can add tints of weak colour to develop line drawings made in pencil or ink. A small box of watercolours or a few tubes of gouache or watercolour paints can therefore extend the scope of your work. Add to these two or three different sized watercolour brushes and a large flat wash brush.

Paper

You will need a stock of good quality cartridge paper. The thickness and quality of paper is indicated by its weight in grams per square metre (gsm).

Sheet sizes are now mostly standardized to ISO (International Organization for Standardization) paper sizes. Each size in the list below is exactly half of the next:

A1   840 × 594 mm
A2   594 × 420 mm
A3   420 × 297 mm
A4   297 × 210 mm

The type of paper will greatly influence the resultant drawing and the way that different tools and media respond.

- 150 gsm cartridge paper will suit most pencil drawings, dry colour drawings in crayon and some ink techniques.
- 220 gsm cartridge paper is best for very soft pencil effects and charcoal work.
- Use a smooth art paper, layout paper or non-bleed marker paper for work in pen and ink, fibre and felt-tip pens.
- Ingres papers and cheaper sugar paper (in various colours) are the most suitable for chalks, pastels and heavier charcoal work.
- 300 gsm watercolour paper is required for washes, brush drawings and tinted and painted work.

Keep samples of a wide range of different papers so that, if necessary, you can do a few tests with any medium prior to drawing. For some wet techniques the paper will need preparing in the way described on page 115.

Paper is said to have a 'right' and a 'wrong' side. Of course, either side can be used, though for most drawings the correct side will be the one with the uneven surface. To check this, hold the sheet up to the light and bend over one corner: one side should have an even, mechanical surface, the other will be uneven.

Additionally, you will need at least one sketchbook. More details about these are given in Chapter 6, page 86.

Some sheets of tracing paper are also useful. You will find it cheaper to buy large sheets of paper and cut them down to size. Store all papers flat.

———— Ancillary equipment ————

The following drawing aids and items of ancillary equipment are essential.

● You will need several types of **eraser**: a wedge-shaped rubber eraser or plastic eraser for general pencil work; a kneaded or putty rubber for charcoal, pastel and similar soft-tone techniques; and a pencil-type typewriter rubber or a slither cut from a larger eraser for creating fine highlights and delicate edges.
● A sharp **craft knife** for sharpening pencils, cutting paper, scratching into wax, etc.
● **Fixative**. Choose ozone-friendly aerosol cans and use in well-ventilated conditions. Spray this on charcoal, pastel and any other drawings which are likely to smudge.
● **Clips and pins**. Use bulldog clips, drawing board clips or drawing pins to secure work while in progress.
● A plastic bevelled-edged **set square** or ruler.
● Metal blowpipe **diffuser**. For simple ink and paint spraying techniques.
● **Paper tissues**, cotton buds and cotton wool. For modifying and blending soft media like pastels and for various paint and texture techniques.
● A roll of 5cm brown **gummed tape**.

- **A drawing board**. Proper art boards are expensive. Buy a sheet of 9mm plywood which is slightly larger than an A2 sheet of paper. You can, of course, have smaller and larger boards as well!

See how your work progresses before buying any other equipment. If you enjoy working outside you may eventually want to buy a sketching easel and folding stool, for example.

Additionally, it is always useful to have a sturdy folio to keep work in or to be able to store it flat on shelves or in a plan chest. If you are fortunate to have your own room, studio or workspace of some description, you can gradually invest in better equipment and work facilities.

Choice of materials

A recommended basic checklist of materials is included on page 3. Try them all out and get to know something of their characteristics and potential. You will find that you like some media more than others. This is fine to begin with while you are learning techniques and gaining confidence. But don't just stick to pencil drawings and do remember that there are many colour drawing techniques.

Although some of the materials will not be put to immediate use, have them ready. Nothing is more frustrating than wanting to try out a particular effect only to find that you do not have the necessary materials in stock!

Your drawings will only improve if you are prepared to take risks and consider new ideas and techniques. Repeating the same old subjects in the same old way will not get you very far. The more experience you have of a wide variety of materials and techniques, the better equipped you will be to choose the best way of expressing your ideas.

Buying materials

Go to a reputable artists' materials shop where you should also be able to get some good advice and test out samples and products you are interested in.

Here is my recommended 'starter' shopping list. You can add to this as the need arises.

- 10 A1 sheets of 150 gsm cartridge drawing paper. You can cut this to any shapes and sizes you need.
- Two A1 sheets of 220 gsm cartridge paper.
- A few sheets of buff, cream, and grey Ingres pastel paper or sugar paper.
- An A4 spiral bound cartridge sketchbook.
- A small notebook with smooth plain paper.
- HB, B, 2B, 4B and 6B drawing pencils.
- Some water-soluble or conté coloured pencils. You can buy them separately, starting with just a few colours to try out.
- A box of stick charcoal and a medium charcoal pencil.
- A small selection of soft pastels. Colours bought separately are cheaper than buying a whole box.
- A box of wax crayons.
- A fine fibre pen (black); a marker pen (black) and a fine mapping pen.
- A small bottle of Indian ink.
- No. 2 and no. 4 watercolour brushes; a no. 6 round hog brush (for stippling – see page 62 – and washes).
- One or two small tubes of gouache or watercolour paints. Just stick to red, yellow and blue to begin with.
- The essential ancillary equipment listed on pages 29–30.

—— Testing out your equipment ——

Now that you have learnt something about the range of drawing materials and have collected a stock of your own it is time to do some testing and experiments. As you work through the different sections of this book you will see that artists are fond of making roughs and preliminary sketches and trying out different ideas and techniques before they make their final decisions for the main drawing. This is a good habit to get into.

Keep all of your drawings for future reference and comparison. Although you may not want to show most of them to anyone else, they are useful in showing you what progress you have made. Media tests and experiments should be labelled to identify which drawing tool or material was used and with one or two brief notes on the effects you tried out.

Now try the projects listed below.

Projects

1 Work through all the drawing media in your collection, starting with
pencils. Using a new A3 sheet for each medium, see what range of
marks, shading effects and textures you can make. Try holding the
drawing tools in different positions and using various pressures. Fill
the sheets with notes and experiments in this way.

My two test pieces using a 6B pencil, shown in illustrations **24** and
25, will give you a starting point. In the first I have varied the angle
and pressure of the pencil to see how this affects the lines I am
drawing, starting with the pencil held vertically and finishing with it
used on its side. The second illustration shows a variety of line
effects, from wavy to hatched.

2 Now combine two or three different media and a range of techniques
in a single drawing, like my abstract in illustration **26**. Use colour if
you wish.

3 Take as your subject some fruit or vegetables, like the onions in
illustration **15**, or a view from your window, as in illustration **13**. Try
drawing it three times, each time using a different media. Compare
the results and decide which drawing works best. Why?

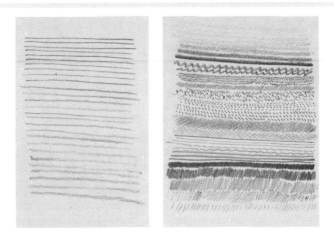

Illustration 24 Practise varying the angle and pressure of the pencil
Illustration 25 Try an exercise like this to test out your pencil and see what
lines and effects are possible

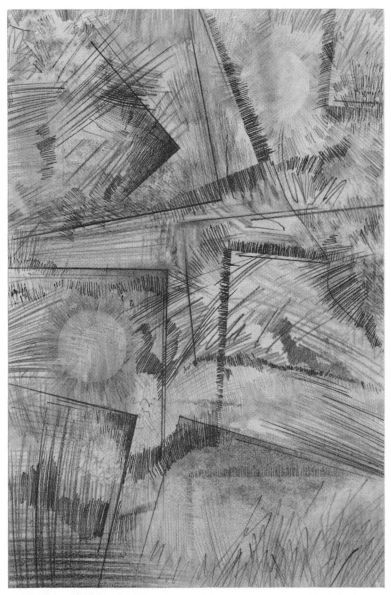

Illustration 26 Experimenting with several media and a range of techniques

3
LOOKING, SEEING AND INTERPRETING

Most of our drawings originate from direct observation: we sit down with the subject in front of us and draw. Usually we want to create a drawing *of* the subject and our aims are realism and accuracy. But sometimes we draw *from* the subject and then we can be more selective and original in our approach.

Before starting any drawing we have to make various decisions. What am I going to draw? How large is the drawing going to be? What medium and technique will be best? What sort of drawing do I want? We set out with certain intentions. As the drawing progresses we may decide to change these intentions and at the end we can judge whether we have succeeded or failed in realising our aims and objectives.

To begin with I shall encourage you to investigate different media, practise the basic techniques and do a lot of carefully observed drawings of a wide variety of subjects. Later, as your own style and ideas about drawing emerge, you will want to draw in a more subjective and personal way. But even those who draw from memory and imagination need the initial discipline of observation and the accumulation of an accurate and extensive visual vocabulary of different shapes and subjects.

However, drawing is much more than acquiring skill with the hand. It requires looking, perceiving and the desire to communicate ideas in a visual way. Confronted with the problem of translating the subject matter before us into a convincing drawing, we must first look and understand. An important part of learning to draw is therefore learning to look and notice things. Drawings do not fail simply because the artist lacks experience in handling a particular technique. Often the failure is due to an inadequate observation of proportions, structure, form, detail, characteristics, and so on. So, artists need to be nosy and enquiring!

You will begin to appreciate that before you can commit any marks to paper, drawing is a constant process of asking questions and reaching decisions. And there are no short cuts. A casual glance at something will merely give you limited information to work from. Get used to looking at everything in a questioning way in order to give yourself plenty of information. Examine everything with a fresh eye, even if it is a shape or subject that you think you know well. Avoid general assumptions or preconceptions. Learn to see one part of the subject in relation to the whole.

To help yourself look at things carefully you should do as much drawing as possible. This is one reason why you should keep a sketchbook and there is more information on this in Chapter 6. You will find that if you are really interested and excited by a subject you are more likely to achieve a good drawing. Attitude and enthusiasm are other important factors influencing your success. Equally, you will need to practise and persevere. Of course, you will not like everything you do, but in a sense you will learn more from your failures than your successes. Don't take too much notice of other people's opinions. There is no single correct way to draw, although many people assume that a drawing is poor if it doesn't look virtually photographic!

There is an underlying emphasis in many parts of this book on looking and seeing. I have stressed the importance of looking in a way which helps you understand the subject so that you can then draw it more accurately. I should not, however, like to give the impression that understanding can only lead to straightforward observation studies. But because such drawings help train the eye as well as the hand, they are ideal for the beginner. As you learn more about drawing you will see that it can also be concerned with expressing your feelings. From the same basis of understanding what you see you can interpret in your own personal way by emphasising certain points or analysing, selecting and developing particular aspects. Now let's look at these various approaches in more detail. Bear in mind that a drawing which concentrates on one of these approaches does not necessarily exclude all the others.

Observation

In many ways drawing and painting are inseparable. Each can be regarded as a distinct discipline in its own right, though it is difficult to define rigid boundaries. Creating a painting often involves a lot of preliminary drawing, just as making a drawing sometimes includes brush and paint techniques. In the past, drawings were mainly considered as essential preparatory work for painting rather than as separate works of art. Most drawings were made as studies, for information and research, or as composition roughs and cartoons. Although the scope and importance of drawing has developed, its original role remains vital. Whether they are employed in preparatory work, in the evolution of designs or in presenting information, drawing skills are essential to all artists, designers and craftspeople. For many, there is still a need to make carefully observed drawings from life.

When we set out to make an accurate likeness of an object or scene before us this is known as working from direct observation. In such

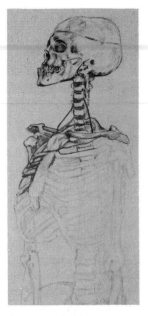

Illustration 27   Working from an underlying structure

drawings we are working objectively, aiming for a true representation without any elaboration, emphasis or selectivity. We need to be inquisitive; the importance of looking, noticing and understanding has already been stressed.

Before you start some observation drawings of your own think about these points:

- The most suitable type of paper and techniques.
- Size and proportion.
- Individual shapes.

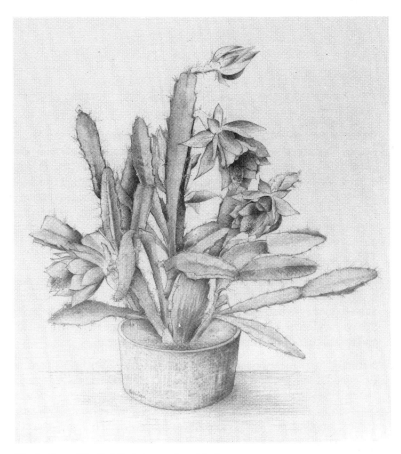

Illustration   28   Detailed observation drawing

- Structure: how are the shapes formed?
- Light and dark.
- Surface textures and details.

Consider these points in relation to illustrations **27** and **28**. The first step in any drawing is roughly to plan it out so as to fit the paper and so that the main shapes are in the correct positions and proportions. Getting a good 'structure' to the drawing is important, so that you can then develop it with confidence. Look at illustration **27** and notice how the structure has been sketched in and the drawing is gradually being worked over with more detail and accuracy. Compare this to the completed pencil drawing in illustration **28** in which various techniques have been used to show different tonal effects, textures and surface details.

Analysis

Observation may, of course, include a certain amount of analysis but it is usually concerned with making a single drawing from a single viewpoint. Sometimes we need more than this and want to examine the subject in greater detail. In such cases a whole series of drawings might be necessary. These could show different viewpoints as well as consider all the factors listed for observation drawings. Alternatively, several drawings could be made from the same viewpoint but with each drawing focusing on a different aspect: form, colour, texture, detail and so on. This will probably require a variety of media and techniques.

Demanding detailed enquiry and entailing a range of drawing skills, analytical drawings therefore provide sound practice for the beginner – indeed, for any artist. Occasionally, it is good really to probe a subject in this way and such drawings will provide valuable preparatory information and research for more elaborate or imaginative works.

Natural forms make ideal subject matter. They can be twisted and examined from various angles and often have interesting colours, details and textures to deal with. Sometimes, like the tomato in illustration **29**, they can be cut open and drawn in sectional view as well. With larger shapes, another possibility is to make a line drawing of the complete shape and then isolate a section for particular analysis, as in illustration **30**.

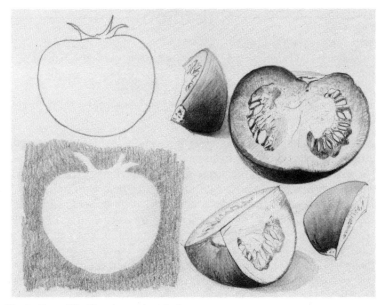

Illustration 29 Drawing and analysis

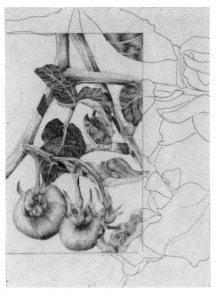

Illustration 30 Analytical study

Selection

Observation and analysis are objective approaches which lead to informative, representational drawings. While these processes are the basis of most of our work, they are not always an end in themselves. As we gain in confidence and skill we may wish to impose a certain personal interpretation on what we see.

None of us sees a subject in quite the same way, even when we are attempting a drawing from direct observation. Our choice of size, viewpoint, medium and technique gives the work a degree of individuality, even here. But we can go further than this: we can select and emphasize those features and characteristics of the subject matter which appeal to us most. Often we are inspired by a subject for a particular reason. We are struck by its dramatic qualities of light and dark, for example, or its interesting shape and form. Therefore we can stress those features in our drawing. We are in fact interpreting what we see, conveying what in our opinion is the essence of the subject by a process of selection.

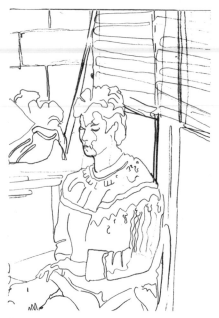

Illustration 31 Selection: line

It is easy to argue that all drawings involve selection to a degree. There has to be some simplification and selection even in the most objective approach. No one is capable of producing a perfect likeness. But, although we might decide to respond in a more individual way to our subject, this will equally derive from first looking and understanding.

Inextricably linked with interpretation is the artist's choice of medium and technique. For an idea involving atmospheric and diffused colour effects, for example, soft pastels would be much more suitable than coloured pencils, which might give a more linear effect. Look at the figure drawing in illustration **31**. Although this is confined to the selective use of line, there is a successful impression of form and space and an interesting composition and interplay of different shapes.

Feeling

Drawings can also show mood and emotion and be created in a subjective and expressive way. Look, for example at the vigorous Van Gogh drawing on page 2. Some artists manage to charge their drawings with great passion and feeling.

The ability to draw with this sort of freedom and sensitivity usually evolves only after a great deal of practice and experience. You need to be accomplished in and confident with different techniques and able to react to a subject in a spontaneous way, rather than with the 'matter of fact' approach of an objective drawing. You have really got to be excited and inspired by an idea; you must really *want* to draw it.

Lively drawings of this type seem to imply a quick method of working and a sort of outpouring of inspiration. This is largely true. Equally, you will not respond to every subject in a passionate way. In many of your drawings you will be looking for a more straightforward approach. But there will be times when you are moved to this sort of response and perhaps experiment with a 'looser' technique.

Medium, subject matter and individual artistic style all play their parts in creating drawings with feeling. Any medium can be used sensitively and expressively but you may find some media, like pastel and charcoal, less inhibiting than others. Be prepared to experiment occasionally. Similarly, try a variety of subjects and ideas. A derelict industrial landscape can be as just inspiring as a moonlit lake. And don't worry about finding a style – this will come in time. Style is something which gradually develops and is influenced by a wide range of things, perhaps from your study of other artists' work or the particular medium and techniques you most often use.

Sketching techniques are a great help in developing quick and more spontaneous methods of drawing. Chapter 6 deals with these in more detail. Illustration **32** is a quick sketch made on the spot using brown conté crayon on toned paper. Here I have attempted to capture the mood and feel of the scene rather than any detailed description.

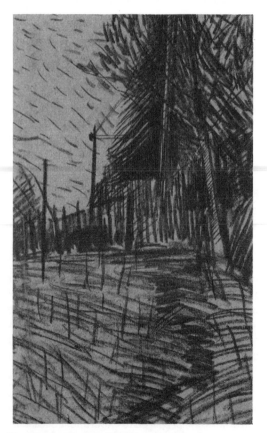

Illustration 32 Showing feeling. Conté on toned paper

Developing

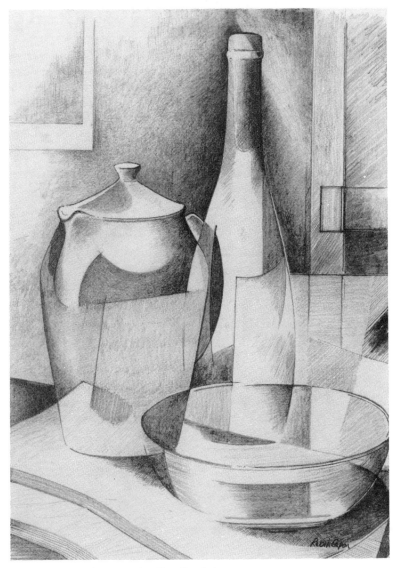

Illustration 33 Interpretation. Pencil techniques

Sometimes the subject before you acts as a sort of starting point or trigger for a more stylized, imaginative or even abstract approach. It provides you with the basis of an idea that you can develop or interpret in an extremely individual way. You might emphasize or exaggerate, distort or simplify. You could decide to use an unusal viewpoint or work in a limited colour or tonal range. There are many possibilities.

Such drawings often result from an intellectual process, that is applying theory or restriction to the way that the work is developed. If you look at my still life drawing in illustration 33 you will see that I have simplified the shapes and areas of tone while at the same time giving equal weight to reflections and overlapping shapes. This process has provided a strong composition and series of shapes to develop with various pencil tonal effects.

Projects

1 Work from a flowering pot plant. Draw from direct observation, making two drawings, each from a different viewpoint. If it is a complex or large plant, concentrate on two different parts of it. Aim for carefully observed drawings which you could send to someone else to show them exactly what the plant looks like.
2 Now try a contrasting approach. Make a third drawing with a stick of charcoal or pastel working quickly, aiming to express the general characteristics of the plant.

4
—— LEARNING ——
THE BASIC
TECHNIQUES

From your initial experiments with different drawing tools and media you can now go on to check the scope of each one with regard to a variety of basic drawing techniques. But first let's clarify what is meant by technique. The term is ambiguous in that it can be applied to both general work in any medium as well as specific methods of applying that medium. For example, charcoal drawing is a general technique, whereas working with tone is a means of manipulating the charcoal to create a particular effect. In this section you will be concentrating on methods rather than media. We shall be considering the main techniques of line, point, tone and texture.

These methods form the most significant part of your foundation course and you will see that this chapter is the largest in the book. It will take you some time to work through because it is vital that you practise every technique until you have some confidence with it. Moreover, it is important that you try out the various techniques with as many different drawing materials as you can. This will give you a good range of basic skills from which to start developing your drawing ideas with real confidence. For most of these methods ordinary cartridge paper will be fine, but notice that for some of the texture and tone ideas you will need a heavier quality paper such as Ingres paper, sugar paper or watercolour paper.

A knowledge of different techniques will mean that you can choose the most suitable method for your subject matter and the particular effects you wish to create. So try out as many of the ideas in this section as you can. Don't worry about wasting time or paper. All the time spent on drawing is helping to develop your skills and understanding of the subject. Keep all your try-outs and experiments for further reference.

—————— Drawing with lines ——————

Line is the most commonly used drawing technique and the most versatile. Most drawing tools are designed to make lines. So you can use lines to show the shape of something, to create light and dark areas and textures, and to suggest different surface effects, like rippling water or windswept grass. Your lines can be delicate and sensitive or bold and expressive. They can be short or long, thick or thin, closely or widely spaced, curved, straight, ruled, freehand, and so on. A line drawing can be a quick sketch or a highly detailed study.

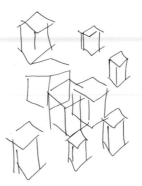

Illustration   34   Drawing with eyes closed!

You may have explored the fundamentals of line in your experiments with various media in Chapter 2. If not, start by seeing what types of line are possible with each of your drawing tools and materials. Refer back to illustrations **24** and **25** for some ideas. Remember that the way you hold and manipulate the medium will affect the sort of lines you get, especially regarding the amount of pressure you use. You could add to these investigations by including some alternative methods of making lines, like the impressed drawing in illustration **22**, offsetting lines with the edge of a piece of card dipped in ink, or erasing lines with the sharp point of a rubber.

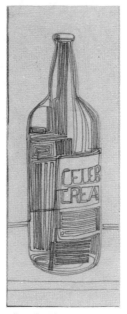

Illustration 35 Continuous line drawing

Outline and simple line drawings can use the economy of line to great effect. Thick bold lines will catch our attention, stand out and appear nearer, while weak, thin lines will give a sense of distance. Many famous artists are renowned for their powerful line drawings, especially Picasso, Matisse, Hockney and Klee. There is a good range of line drawings included in this book, so in conjunction with those found on the next few pages, have a look also at illustrations **9, 19, 31, 78, 84—87, 93, 98, 100** and **148**.

Illustrations **34—36** are fun ideas though nevertheless entirely valid in helping to develop line techniques and confidence in handling different drawing tools. I can draw cubes better than those shown in illustration **34**, but make allowances for the fact that I had my eyes closed for this drawing! Try it for yourself. This technique gives you good practice in visualising a shape in a very concentrated way as well as making positive lines in the right places.

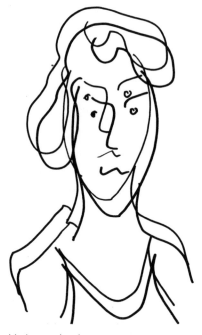

Illustration 36 Double-image drawing

Sometimes drawings work much better if you stick to a few self-imposed rules. Such 'rules' will give a unity and impact to the work, qualities which are often lacking when the drawing is allowed to become complicated by involving too many ideas and techniques. So, when using lines, for example, keeping to a single type of line frequently works best. Try doing a drawing, like my bottle in illustration **35**, which is made up of a single, continuous line. This will test your imagination and ingenuity! Start at the top and do not remove your pen or pencil until the drawing is finished. You are allowed to backtrack over lines already drawn! In illustration **36** I tried holding two pens together – getting a sort of double image effect. See if you can think of any other 'fun' methods like these.

Outline drawing, like the view in illustration **37**, is a splendid technique for sketchbook work and preliminary studies. The essence of an idea can be captured in a few, well-chosen lines, using variations of emphasis to suggest some space and depth. Try drawing different objects in your room in this way, perhaps in charcoal and fibre pen, as well as pencil.

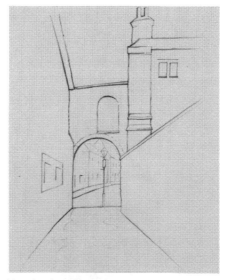

Illustration 37   Line drawing. Fibre pen

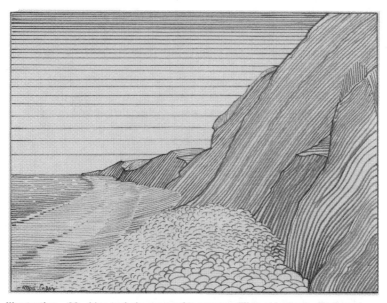

Illustration 38   Line techniques used to convey different textures, depth and direction

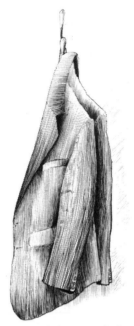

Illustration 39 Line drawing: texture and tone. Ball-point pen

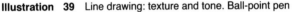

Surfaces can be modelled and different textures implied by using lines of various types and applying them with particular sensitivity and direction, as in illustration **38**. Additionally, lines can suggest light and dark areas by varying their proximity. Notice how, in illustration **39**, the heavier, closely-spaced lines give dark shadows, while the weaker, more open lines create highlights and soft tones. In this drawing the line technique is totally effective, for it combines a sense of form and tone with something of the texture and characteristics of this particular subject.

Summary points

- Lines can be drawn with most drawing tools and materials.
- Use variations of pressure to create lines of different strength and intensity.
- Lines can suggest three-dimensional form, tone, textures and surface characteristics.
- Lines are good for outline drawings, sketchbook techniques, preliminary studies and composition roughs.
- You can combine lines with any other technique.

—————— Using guidelines ——————

When we want to draw something very accurately it is usually a good idea to start with some faint guidelines to help us position things correctly and get the right shapes and sizes. The sequence of illustrations on the next few pages shows how guidelines can be useful in establishing a basic structure for the drawing. They give us a sort of skeleton over which the accurate shapes can be evolved. To work in this way you must become accustomed to looking analytically and understanding which essential lines will provide the clues for the final drawing.

It can be argued that these construction lines, although aiding accuracy, give a rigidity and coldness to the work. Obviously this is a formal approach to drawing and worked as a step-by-step process it will hinder spontaneity and flow. However, there are many occasions in still-life compositions and general planning where a few quick guidelines can aid the way forward, with subsequent work developed as freely as you wish. Also, for beginners, it is sound practice to learn reliable ways of drawing cylindrical, symmetrical and similar basic shapes. Like perspective and other devices, once the theory is fully understood it will automatically influence the work without the necessity of going through all the guideline stages.

Study illustrations **40** to **47** and try out these ideas for yourself. For the moment I want you to concentrate on learning how to pick out the bare bones of a drawing, as well as practising the construction of ellipses, cylinders and symmetrical shapes in the way I have shown. Obviously this work is interrelated to perspective, a subject which is dealt with in detail in the next chapter. You will also see that guidelines feature in other drawings in this book. Have a look at illustrations **6, 27, 74—76, 80, 81, 93** and **119**.

Once you have mastered these basic shapes you can apply the same procedure to more complex objects. Box shapes are very much influenced by perspective, so I have considered these in that context in the next chapter. Start by practising some curved lines, for example, illustration **40a**. Draw from inside the curve with a free-flowing action of the hand. If you are right-handed your curves will flow from left to right; if you are left-handed do the opposite. The action is from the wrist: try it with curves of different lengths and in different media. Think of an ellipse as a squashed circle. The degree to which it is squashed depends on your viewpoint: the higher your viewpoint, the more circular the ellipse.

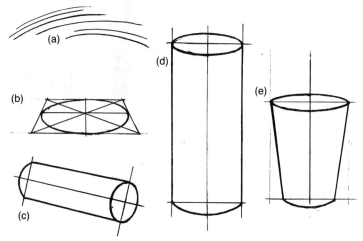

Illustration 40   Constructing ellipses and cylinders

Notice how in **40b** ellipses can be constructed using a grid of lines. Notice, too, that the ellipse fits into a square which is distorted by viewpoint and consequently perspective. For this reason, the front half of the ellipse, being nearer to you, must be made slightly bigger than the back half.

Cylinders (**40d**) and similar shapes (**40c**) can be based on a rectangle constructed to fit the estimated proportions of width to height. Central guidelines are used to help ensure that the shape is balanced and to plot out the ellipses. For a shape like **40e** start with a rectangle based on the widest dimension, in this case the top, and then estimate the angles of the sides. A common fault is to 'point' ellipses at each side. Remember that it is easier and more natural to draw from inside the curve, so turn your paper upside down to draw the nearer half of the ellipse. Think of it as a continuous line – no points.

For a cylinder/tube shape which is lying on its side fix the centre lines, as in illustration **40c**, and note that the main rectangular shape is distorted by perspective as it recedes. These centre lines are also known as 'axis lines', particularly when they show the angle and direction of the basic shape, as here. See also illustration **119**. Now practise all of the shapes in illustration **40** for yourself.

Many shapes are symmetrical, that is, equally balanced either side of the centre, or are basically symmetrical, with something added, like a handle.

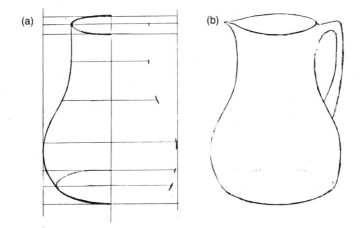

Illustration   41   Constructing symmetrical shapes

Once again, such shapes can be plotted either side of a central guideline, as in illustration **41a**. Begin with a rectangle based on the maximum width and height. Put in a central line and draw one side of the shape. Notice where the shape changes direction and estimate such points in proportion to the whole. If you are right-handed, like me, you will find it easier to draw the left-hand half of the shape. When you are satisfied with this, draw some guidelines across at key points where the outline alters. You can mark off a point on these lines which is the same distance from the centre as the corresponding point on the opposite side. Like my drawing in illustration **41**, create a series of these points which you can then join up to establish the other half of the shape. Rub out the unwanted faint guide lines and modify the main shape as necessary (**41b**).

For other objects use as many or as few guidelines as seem necessary to help you build up an accurate outline. This general principle is demonstrated in the step-by-step drawings in illustrations **42–44**. From the basic framework you can get a good outline drawing and then add detail and tone.

Initial guidelines are especially helpful when planning a composition like the one shown in illustration **45**. Here you need to fix the overall scale of the work before locating the position and shape of each object and its position and proportion relative to the others. Guidelines are fine for checking angles and proportions. Look at the contrasting approaches in illustrations **46** and **47**.

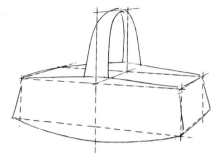

Illustration 42 Using guidelines

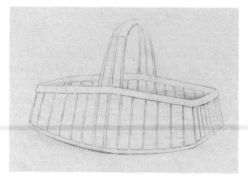

Illustration 43 Foundation line drawing

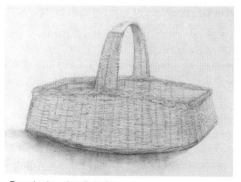

Illustration 44 Developing detail and tone

Use guidelines for:

- Plotting particular shapes and measurements, especially symmetrical shapes.
- Checking the position of one thing in relation to another.
- Planning overall scale and composition.

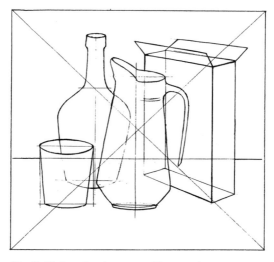

Illustration   45   Guidelines for shapes, positions, scale

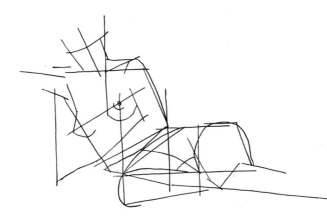

Illustration   46   Plotting form with guidelines

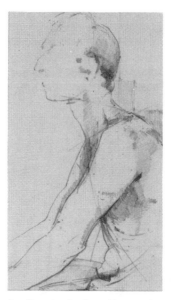

Illustration 47 Extending lines to check positions and proportions

——————— Drawing with point ———————

Soft pencils and most pens are suitable for this technique, especially fine, fibre-tipped pens, ball-point pens, art pens, and technical pens like those made by Rotring and Staedtler which use interchangeable nibs of various thicknesses. Use the instrument vertically and pounce it up and down to produce dots or hold it at a slight angle if you want to achieve little stabs of tone. Usually it is possible to create slight variations of light and dark by varying the pressure. Also, of course, you can combine different drawing tools, although it is best to do a few tests first to check their compatibility. Some pens use a much more intense ink than others. Equally, exciting drawings are possible by using a range of coloured pencils, the softer conté pencils generally proving the most suitable. Your experiments with this technique might also reveal that you can make dots and dashes by other means: offsetting from a drinking straw, a thin piece of dowel or the blunt end of a paintbrush dipped in ink, for example.

It has to be said that making a drawing entirely with dots can be a time-consuming and rather repetitive process. On the other hand, the broken texture and tone effects are unusual and visually very interesting. This is a method which is particularly good for exploring subtle variations of light and dark, as in my woodland study in illustration **48**. Here I used a fine fibre-tip pen exploiting different pressures and spacing to vary the intensity of the tones. Like many of the 'pointillist' drawings by Van Gogh, Signac and Seurat, point combines well with linear techniques.

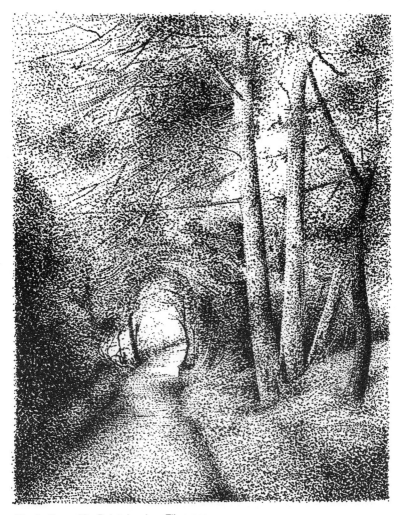

Illustration   48   Point drawing. Fibre pen

—————— Wash and spray effects ——————

Wash is drawing ink or water-based paint heavily diluted in water. Mix the wash in an old saucer, shallow container or plastic palette, starting with a few drops of ink or colour and then adding plenty of clean water. Try the wash on some scrap paper to test its strength: add more colour or water as necessary.

Wash is normally applied sparingly with a large, soft brush to tint areas of a line drawing, like the pen and wash study shown in illustration **49**. You can use various strengths or colours, or work over parts with several layers of wash until the correct strength is obtained (see illustration **50**). Work on good quality cartridge paper, preferably stretched (see page 115). Your main drawing can be in almost any medium, but bear in mind that most felt-tip and fibre-tip pens as well as soft media, like charcoal and pastel, are not permanent. This means that they will fuzz or run if wetted with wash, although this can be an advantage, depending on the subject matter and the sort of effects desired. Pencil and Indian ink lines are more permanent.

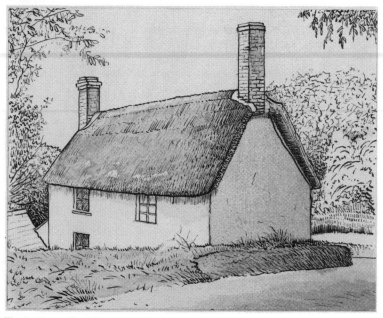

Illustration 49 Line and wash study. Ink

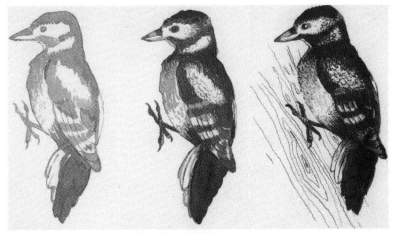

Illustration 50 Wash drawing. Poster paint

This is a technique which also suits general background effects, perhaps tinting the whole paper prior to drawing. In addition, you can use wash over a resist medium such as wax or masking fluid. Brushed over wax, the wash will produce an interesting texture (see illustration **53**), while masking fluid is useful for blocking out specific shapes and details. With large areas of wash you must work quickly to avoid any premature drying and the consequent uneven patches. Use the largest brush possible.

Ink and thin paint can also be sprayed on to a drawing, like the background effect in illustration **51** which, incidentally, uses some brush and wash techniques also. I used a cheap metal spray diffuser for this and some Indian ink. Similar effects are achieved using a spattering method from an old toothbrush or stiff-haired hog brush. Load the brush with ink or paint, hold it directly in front of the selected part of the drawing, pull back the bristles with your forefinger, and as they spring back they will shower the drawing with fine spray. An airbrush can also be used for this work. While it is far more reliable and controllable, it is an expensive item of equipment and is not worth purchasing unless required frequently.

With diffuser and airbrush techniques you will need to mask out certain parts of the drawing to prevent them receiving any spray, and covering the immediate vicinity with newspapers for the same reason! Small details can be blocked out with masking fluid, otherwise use specific shapes cut from paper and fixed to the drawing with Blu-Tack. In my picture in illustration **51** the circular shape of the moon was retained as white in this way. Because it wasn't too intrusive, I could work over some

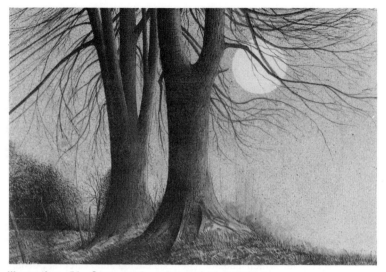

Illustration 51 Spray, wash, and various ink techniques

parts of the spray with a pen and ink, but sometimes it is necessary to identify specific areas to spray. When you have sketched in your composition, make a tracing of those parts which must not be sprayed. Transfer the traced out shapes on to thin paper, then cut them out and fix them to the drawing in the manner already described. Make some test sprays first. Tilt the drawing at a slight angle, then spray in light coatings, building up the intensity of the tone or colour you require. The further back from the drawing you stand, the finer will be the spray.

——————— Using texture ———————

Look around and you will see that many subjects involve texture – that is a particular surface quality. Some things are completely smooth while others are grained, rippled, woven, indented, furry and so on. Wood, like the fencing slats in illustration **52**, is an obvious example.

If you want your drawing to show a good likeness of something then one of your aims must be convincingly to reproduce the surface characteristics. However, although most drawing media can be handled so as to suggest texture, a drawing cannot have the same tactile qualities as a

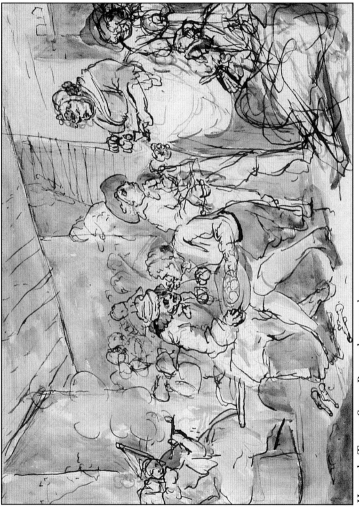

Hogarth, *Tavern Scene*. Pen and watercolour.

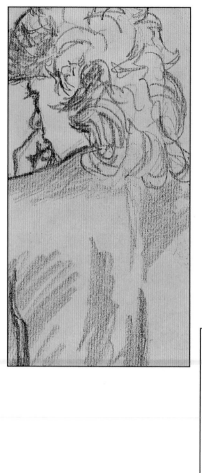

(left) Line drawing. Pastel on toned paper.

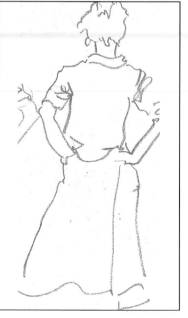

(right) Line drawing. Pastel.

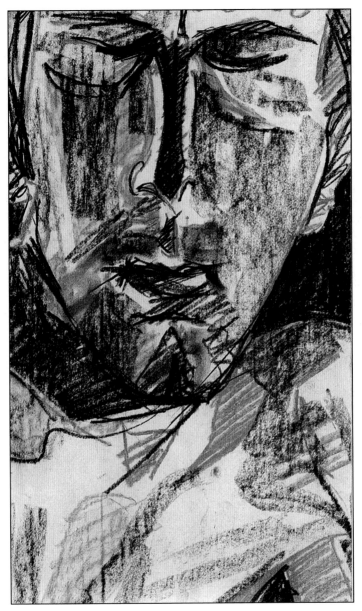

Portrait study. Pastel.

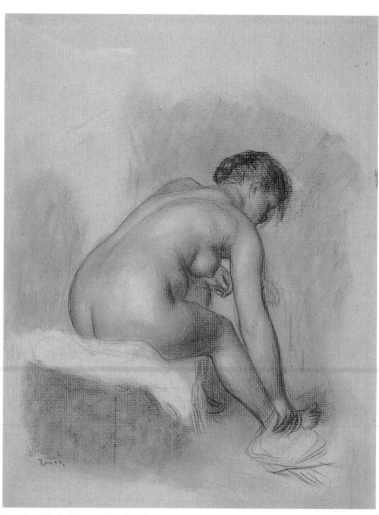

Renoir, *Nude Woman Drying her Foot*. Red chalk heightened with white.
Reproduced by courtesy of the Trustees of The British Museum.

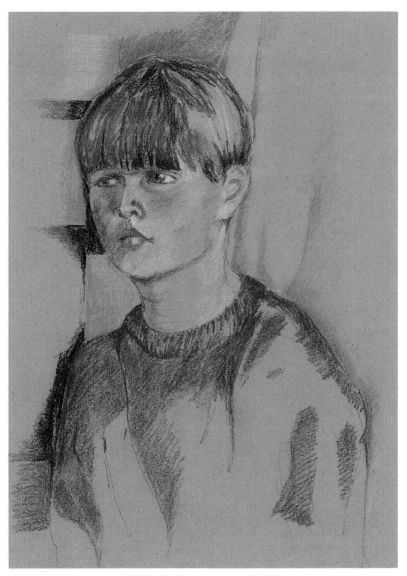

Portrait study. Pastel.

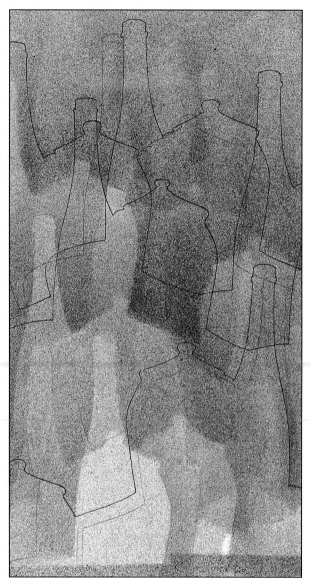

Still life design worked from paper templates. Sprayed ink enhanced with coloured pencil and fibre pen lines.

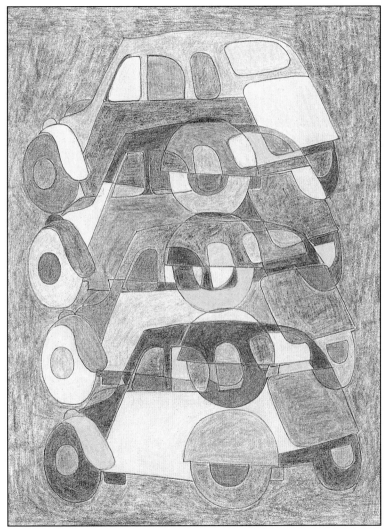

Design made by repeating a shape using a tracing. Coloured pencils.

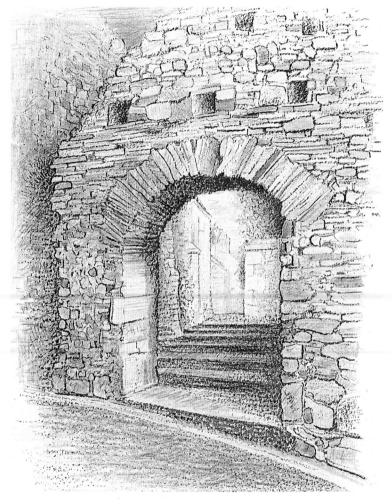

Location study made in charcoal pencil and developed with *conté aquarelle* pencils.

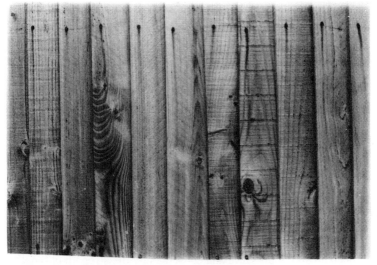

Illustration 52 Texture

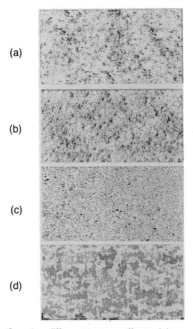

(a)

(b)

(c)

(d)

Illustration 53 Creating different texture effects: (a) sponge; (b) stipple; (c) spattering; (d) resist

painting. As we cannot build up impasto effects, we have to create the *impression* of texture.

You may have already discovered various ways of creating texture effects with different media, perhaps accidentally through experiments. Drawing in line and point will have shown that short lines (hatched) and cross-hatched lines will suggest texture, as will a dotting technique. Look again at illustrations **38** and **48** (pages 49 and 57). Spraying, spattering, stippling and offsetting are other ways of creating textures. Dragging the side of a stick of charcoal, conté or pastel across a sheet of heavy quality paper will also give interesting effects.

Get a feel for textures by first trying out some of the techniques listed below. Then look at the pencil techniques shown in illustrations **54–56**.

- **Rubbings**. Use thin drawing paper and place it over a textured surface like wood grain, a metal grille or frosted glass. Using a short length of wax crayon on its side, shade over the area, gradually building up the pressure and consequently the strength of tone.
- **Sponge**. Dip a small piece of sponge into some ink or paint and lightly press it down on the paper. This will give a blotchy texture, as in **53a**.
- **Stipple**. Use an old stiff-haired brush dipped in a shallow quantity of ink or paint. With just a little liquid on the brush, dab it up and down to produce the sort of mottled effect shown in **53b**.
- **Spattering**. Make a fine spray by dipping an old toothbrush or stiff-haired brush into some ink or paint. Prop the paper up almost vertically. Hold the brush a little distance from the paper and pull back the bristles with your forefinger. See illustration **53c**.
- **Resist**. Coat the paper with a thick layer of wax crayon – a candle works just as well. Paint over this with watercolour or diluted ink. See **53d**.

All of these methods can be worked over, using the same process or another technique, to create stronger tones or different colours.

Although you might only use such methods very occasionally, they can introduce a lively contrast in a drawing. On the other hand, pencil techniques will be called upon much more frequently. In illustration **54** the bolder lines of texture were drawn over preliminary general shading. A 6B pencil was used and notice how there is a mixture of longer lines, hatching, short dabs of tone and a sort of scribble. Each of the still life objects in illustration **55** has a different kind of surface so I have had to invent pencil textures to suit these, varying from dots and dashes to soft areas of tone. A good way of creating an overall feeling of texture is to

work on a heavy quality watercolour paper. You will need to draw with a
soft medium like pastel, charcoal or charcoal pencil, as in illustration **56**.

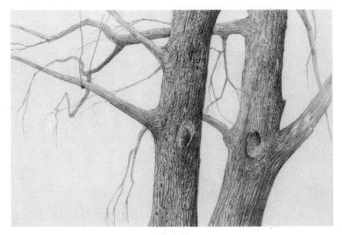

Illustration   54   Interpreting texture. Pencil

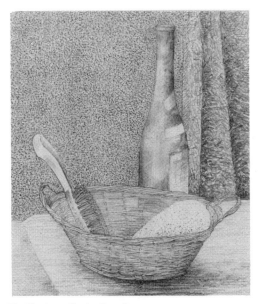

Illustration   55   Texture effects. Pencil

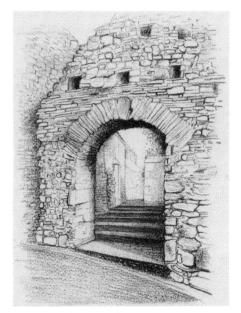

Illustration 56 Using heavily textured paper

—————— Working with tone ——————

Tone is the variations of light and dark in a drawing and is used to help suggest depth and three-dimensional form. Each drawing medium or tool has its own range of tone and certain tonal characteristics. In some, like felt-pens, the degree of variation is limited, while in others, like charcoal or soft pencil, there can be an extensive range from subtle lights to intense darks. With most media, variations of tone are achieved by altering the pressure applied. Get used to handling different media in this way so that you know what tonal effects they can give. In some of your drawings you might need to combine several media in order to create the right contrasts in tone and surface characteristics.

Test out media and shading techniques in the way demonstrated in illustration **57**. Try the same sequence of exercises, then see if you can find other methods, perhaps using different media. Remember that the type of paper is important: use cartridge paper for pencil work, a smooth art paper for fine pens, and sugar paper or a heavier quality paper (Ingres, watercolour, etc.) for charcoal.

- **Linear tone**. The spacing and strength of the lines is important. Notice that heavier lines used close together give a darker effect.
- **Hatched lines**. Use short, crisp lines at an angle of about 45°. Again, the spacing will determine the intensity of the tone.
- **Cross hatching**. Work as for hatching then cover with a series of lines in the opposite direction. This creates a more solid tone effect.

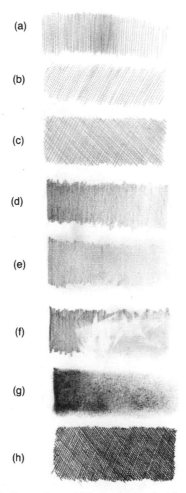

(a)

(b)

(c)

(d)

(e)

(f)

(g)

(h)

Illustration 57 Tone effects: (a) linear; (b) hatched lines; (c) cross-hatching; (d) pressure; (e) blended; (f) erased; (g) charcoal; (h) pen lines

- **Pressure**. Use a soft pencil (3B–6B). Hold the pencil almost horizontally so that the side of the lead is used. Start with very heavy pressure and gradually reduce this so that your shading goes from very dark to light. Try to achieve this without any obvious gaps or lines.
- **Blended**. Use a soft pencil in the same way as in illustration **57d** but this time aim for a more subtle effect by working the tone into the surface of the paper a little. Do this by gently smudging it with a small piece of paper or cloth.
- **Erased**. You can make highlights by removing patches of tone with an eraser. Putty rubbers and other soft erasers can also be used for blending.
- **Charcoal**. This is very good for variations of pressure and blended effects.
- **Pen**. Fine pens will suit line techniques such as hatching, point and other ideas, like the circular, almost scribbled tone effect in illustration **58**.

When you draw from direct observation make a careful assessment of the source and direction of light, the consequent extent and distribution of shadows, and the general tonal 'key' of the subject. It could be that it is evenly lit and therefore there are few darks of any significance. Alternatively, a strong light from a particular direction will cause positive shadows and perhaps many variations of tone. Draw a simple object to try out these differences.

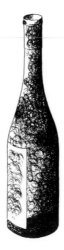

Illustration 58 Scribbled tone

Tone, like many aspects of drawing, will generally work best if it is simplified. If you half close your eyes it often helps to identify the main light or dark areas. To begin with, think in terms of three main tones: dark, medium, and light. Try a drawing which restricts tone in this way, like my still life in illustration **59**.

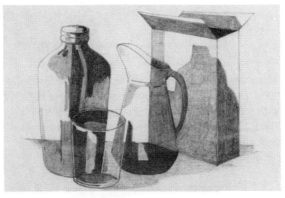

Illustration   59   Keeping to three tones

Hatching techniques are used in illustration **60**. Hard pencils produce a lighter tone than soft ones, so here I have combined several types of pencil to help achieve different tones. The tennis ball in illustration **61** is drawn with a 6B pencil varying the pressure as necessary and keeping the pencil really sharp for the more defined lines.

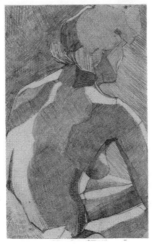

Illustration   60   Hatched tone

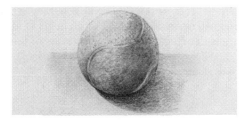

Illustration 61 Variations of pressure to create different tones. Soft pencil

Tone and shape work together to give us a real likeness of something. Sometimes the shape is confused by the great range of light and textures which adorn it. So think in terms of shape first, as in illustration **62**, before tackling the modelling and detail, as in illustration **63**. This example combines various pencil shading methods: solid tone, variations of pressure, blended tone and erased highlights.

Illustration 62 Looking at shape and mass

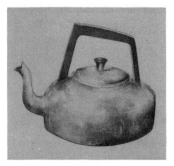

Illustration 63 Combining different pencil shading techniques

——————— Using mixed media ———————

As you work through this section and try out the techniques of line, point, texture and tone with different drawing tools and materials you will begin

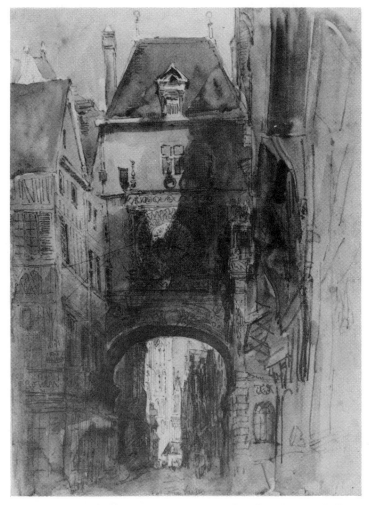

Illustration 64 *Tour d'Horloge, Rouen* by David Cox. Pencil and wash. Tate Galley, London

to realise the potential for combining media. Often a single medium is most effective and will be ideal for a particular subject. However, as you have seen with texture and tone, occasionally it is necessary to combine several media within the same drawing in order to get the most convincing result. Additionally, mixed media effects will give lively contrasts and add to the interest of the drawing.

So, don't be afraid to experiment with a combination of drawing tools and materials in order to increase the scope of your drawing and interpret surfaces in the best way. Remember to check the suitability of your drawing paper to the range of media you intend using. If you have doubts about individual media or techniques, test them out on some scrap paper before using them in the actual drawing. You might include some media specifically because they allow you to draw in detail, while others give you the textures and tones you want or add to the general vitality and atmosphere of the drawing.

Try these ideas:

- Using a range of hard to soft graphite pencils.
- A pencil drawing with added wash (see illustration **64**).
- An Indian ink drawing with colour washes of watercolour.
- A brush drawing developed with charcoal.
- A tonal study using soft pencil, charcoal and charcoal pencil.

—— Matching medium to method ——

It follows that the choice of medium must suit the techniques you have decided to use in your drawing. You would not choose to make a fine line drawing with a thick stick of charcoal, for example, just as you would not expect great delicacy of tone from a felt marker pen. Medium and technique are interlinked. As you gain experience with different drawing materials you will get to know their individual capabilities and characteristics and what range of techniques and effects they allow. Equally, experience will help you judge at the outset of a drawing which media to choose to give you the interpretation and impact you want.

Projects

1   Assemble a still life group consisting of four or five kitchen objects.
    Select them carefully to give a variety of shapes and sizes as well as
    contrasting surfaces (textures). Arrange them into an interesting
    composition. Make a drawing on an A2 sheet of paper which:

    • Plots the accurate position and shape of each object as well as the
      overall scale of the drawing. Refer to illustration **45** (page 55).
    • Develops the required light and dark qualities. Refer to illustra-
      tion **63** (page 68).
    • Includes texture effects where necessary. Refer to illustration
      55 (page 63).
    • Uses more than one medium. Refer to illustration **64** (page 69).

2   Using a different, appropriate medium for each one, make:

    • An outline drawing of a telephone.
    • A study in line and point of part of a garden.
    • A colour study of an apple.
    • A drawing in tone of a collection of cylindrical objects.
    • A careful drawing of a piece of bark or heavily grained wood.

5
—— SIZE AND SCALE ——

Whether your drawing consists of a single subject or a variety of objects and forms, it is likely that you will want to create a convincing impression of space and distance. As well as assessing the correct proportions of individual shapes, you will need to deal with the difficult problems created by objects which recede at an acute angle, make judgements about the relative scale of things, and maybe suggest great depth, as in a landscape view. Artists have always had this problem of creating the illusion of three-dimensional space on a canvas or a sheet of paper which, of course, is two-dimensional. So you will need to know how to use perspective, check proportions, draw foreshortened shapes and imply distance through changes of scale.

—————————— Perspective ——————————

Perspective is a drawing device which helps you suggest depth and space, particularly in relation to straight lines and parallel lines which go back into the distance. While the theory of perspective must be thoroughly understood, most artists do not draw with lots of vanishing points and parallel lines! This would make a drawing look rather artificial and mechanical. Perspective often has to be used in conjunction with other things, like proportion, tone and detail. But you do need to practise the exercises using perspective in illustrations **68–70** and let it influence your work when necessary. Learn to draw with a consciousness of

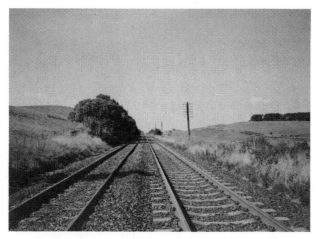

Illustration   65   Perspective in action

perspective, what it does and how it affects certain shapes. Guidelines can sometimes help, but they need not be drawn with laser precision once you have understood what happens in perspective.

Study illustration **65**. The railway lines recede into the far distance. They are parallel lines, yet they appear to converge to a distant point. This demonstrates perspective perfectly: all straight lines and parallel lines

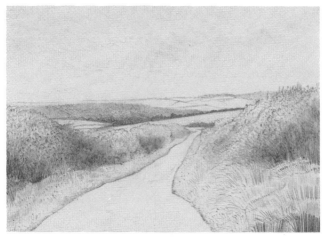

Illustration   66   Using perspective to convey distance

going away from you must be drawn like the railway track. The lines must taper inwards as they go back. If you were to draw them as they really are, in other words keep them the same distance apart, they would look as though they were going up in the air rather than going back into the distance: vertical rather than horizontal. My country lane drawing in illustration **66** is based on the same principle. Although in reality the sides of the road are not exactly parallel, they are drawn so that they get closer together as they recede. This gives a good feeling of distance.

This point is further demonstrated in illustrations **67** and **68**. In the first, the box is drawn with its sides being the same width from front to back: the top and bottom edges are consequently parallel. This is known as an isometric drawing – useful for designers, who need to give accurate measurements. However, there is no sense of depth; in fact, the sides give an optical distortion which makes them look bigger at the back. In illustration **68** however, the box is drawn in perspective, its sides therefore sloping back. This gives a much more convincing sense of form and depth. Notice that vertical lines are unaffected by perspective.

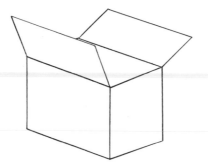

Illustration   67   Box: isometric drawing

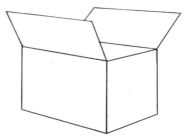

Illustration   68   Box: perspective drawing

In connection with perspective, get to know these terms:

- **Eye-level**. The actual or imagined horizontal line in a drawing which represents your line of vision in relation to the subject, i.e. the height at which your eyes observe the subject. To illustrate this, hold a pencil horizontally about 20cm in front of your eyes.
- **Horizon**. This is always at eye-level – the line where sky meets ground.
- **Converging lines**. Parallel lines influenced by perspective; they appear to get closer together and eventually meet.
- **Vanishing point**. The point where the lines of perspective seem to meet.
- **Centre of vision**. The point on the horizon immediately in front of you as you make the drawing. This is not necessarily the middle of the drawing, because your viewpoint could be from one side.

Now see how perspective affects the shape of things by studying illustrations **69** and **70**. In illustration **69** the table is drawn in what is known as 'one-point' or 'parallel' perspective. Our viewpoint is directly on to one side and from the centre of that side. Note that lines in the drawing which are parallel to the edges of the drawing (that is, horizontal and vertical lines) remain parallel and unaffected by perspective, which only influences receding lines. Therefore, only the two ends of the table are affected, causing the size of the back legs and the far side to appear smaller than those parts nearer to us.

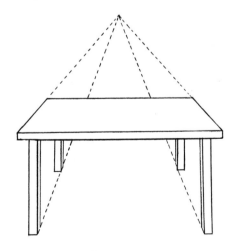

Illustration   69   Parallel perspective

Now consider the alternative views of the house shown in illustration **70**. Here we can see two sides of an object set at an angle to us. Both sides slope back from us into the distance and therefore both are influenced by perspective – in this case what is called 'angular' or 'two-point' perspective. We have two sets of converging lines, each set meets at a vanishing point on the horizon or eye-level line. Look at each sketch in turn:

- **Close-up view (70a).** Here the viewpoint is from normal eye-level but quite close to the building. The depth of the building is contracted or foreshortened and has to be suggested in a very limited space. The distortion of the sides is thus enhanced and the vanishing points consequently quite near the object.
- **Distant view (70b).** The further back we stand the less distortion there is: the sides slope back at less of an angle.
- **Worm's-eye view (70c).** If you squat down or take a very low viewpoint, your eye-level/horizon is consequently lower. The angle of the converging lines of perspective get steeper the further they are above the horizon.
- **Bird's-eye view (70d).** Similarly, if you look from a tall building or the top of a ladder, or work at an easel looking down on a still life group, your viewpoint is from above and the eye-level line is consequently high. You will, therefore, see more of the tops of objects.

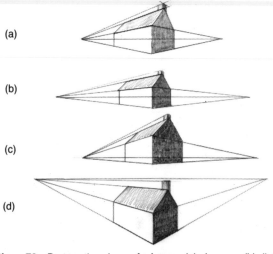

(a)

(b)

(c)

(d)

Illustration 70 Perspective views of a house: (a) close-up; (b) distant; (c) worm's-eye view; (d) bird's-eye view

The best way of appreciating these points is to make some drawings of your own. Project 1 on page 85 will give you some ideas.

● **Remember** to use perspective on objects which have straight lines or parallel sides running back into the distance. This could be a building, a brick wall, a gate or a road, and so on.

Normally you won't draw in the lines of perspective, but you could use a few guidelines. If you were to construct every drawing accurately, as in illustration **70**, then you would either have to scale the objects down tremendously in order to fit all the vanishing points on your paper, or you would have to use enormous sheets of paper! But where you have a subject which is obviously influenced by perspective, give some thought to how lines converge and how this will help you suggest depth and dimension.

—— Comparing shapes and sizes ——

Imagine your sheet of drawing paper as a kind of window frame or the proscenium arch of the theatre. The viewer will look into your drawing in the same sort of way. Therefore, you have to create the illusion of space and depth. Like the set of a traditional stage play or the backdrops of a music hall, think of your drawing as having a series of vertical, receding picture planes. So, as you build up the drawing you need to be constantly aware of how the part you are working on relates to the rest of the composition. You must get each part of the drawing in the right scale and the right place. Therefore, you must make frequent cross-references.

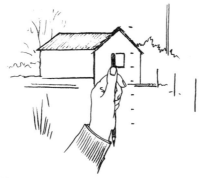

Illustration 71 Measuring relative proportions

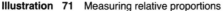

One way of checking relative sizes and positions is to use your pencil as a measuring stick. Do this in the way shown in illustration **71**. Hold your pencil at arm's length and keep your arm straight. With one eye closed, line up the pencil with the edge, distance or angle you wish to check. Align your pencil so that its end corresponds to one end of the distance to be measured, using your thumb to mark the other end. Keeping your arm straight, you can now compare this measurement or angle with a similar or relevant one somewhere else in the composition. In this way you can make a series of comparative checks and measurements to help you draw things in the correct relative scale.

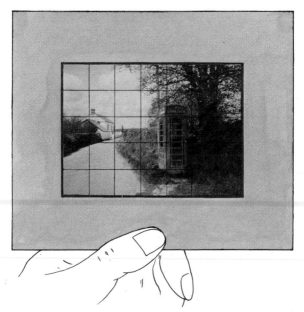

Illustration 72 Using a grid viewfinder to check positions and scale

An alternative is to use a viewfinder which incorporates a grid, as in illustration **72**. This is made as a cardboard frame with an aparture of, say, 10cm × 14cm. You can use clear perspex in the opening, with the grid lines drawn on, or make the grid by gluing lengths of cotton to the back. The squares on the grid will correspond to similar, though larger, squares on your drawing paper. Hold the viewfinder at arm's length in one hand while you map in the essential lines of your drawing using the other hand. You may need to have smaller or larger viewfinders depending on the subject matter and the scale of working.

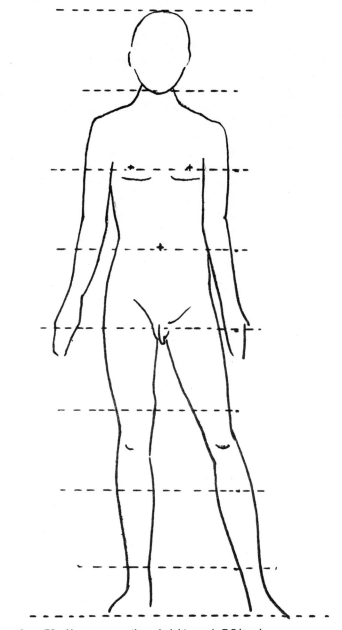

Illustration   73   Human proportions: height equals 7.5 heads

In many individual subjects, like the human figure in illustration **73**, it is essential to estimate the scale of one part correctly in relation to the rest, in other words to get it in the right proportions. Get used to looking at things in this way and noticing whether one part is bigger or smaller than another, and if so by how much. You can use the pencil measuring technique (illustration **71**) to compare different sizes. As you gain experience you will begin to assess proportions automatically in the way that you look and analyse. The more you practise drawing something, the more you will appreciate the proportions involved. This especially applies to the human form. While you should not become lured into the false assumption that every human being fits a certain formula regarding scale and proportion, you can use truths about average people as a guide. In illustration **73**, for example, you will notice that the height of Mr Average is equivalent to 7.5 heads. Notice, too, how dividing the height into 'heads' helps you fix other positions and proportions. With moving figures you might evolve the final drawing from quick matchstick or skeleton sketches, like those in illustration **74**. These can only be drawn quickly and convincingly if you have a knowledge and understanding of basic proportions. Similar points apply to drawing the head (see illustrations **75** and **76**). From a profile view you will see that the head is quite square in overall dimensions, while from a frontal view it is more rectangular. Notice how the features all fit into the lower half of the head.

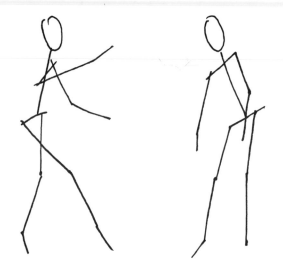

Illustration 74 Developing pose and proportions from stick figures

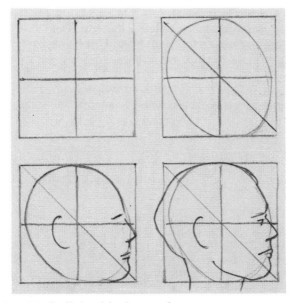

Illustration 75   Profile head: basic proportions

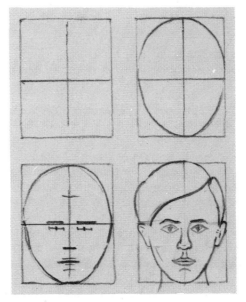

Illustration 76   Head: frontal view proportions

In some views, changing scale and proportions are linked to perspective. Together they give a tremendous sense of distance. This can be further enhanced by the way we use tone and colour. Usually weaker tones and colours are used in the distance and stronger ones with bolder lines for foreground detail and emphasis. Illustration **77** combines all of these methods and you will see that as well as creating a good sense of depth, the various contrasts of scale and tone add interest and variety to the drawing.

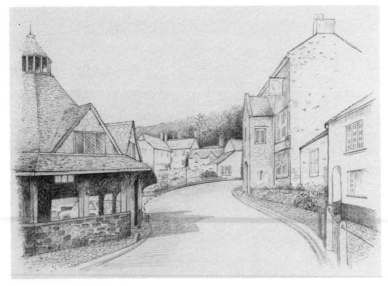

Illustration 77 Using a combination of drawing techniques to create depth: perspective, changing scale, tone, and foreground detail

The position and scale of things is very important when you have to deal with an unusual or exaggerated viewpoint, like something which juts straight out at you. Here, because of its relative position to you, the size and shape of something may be greatly distorted or condensed, an aspect of drawing known as 'foreshortening'. Particularly if you want to convey a lot of distance in a very confined space, you need to use an emphasised perspective. Look at illustration **78** to see how these points apply. In the drawing on the left the lamp is pointing away from us and consequently the lampshade is relatively small in relation to the rest because it is the furthest part from us. Contrastingly, in the right-hand drawing, the lamp shade is closest to us and appears much larger.

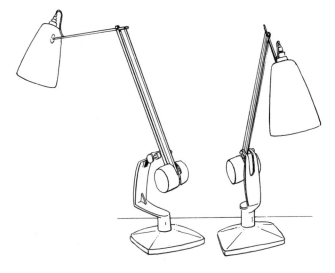

Illustration 78 Foreshortening

– Making your drawings fit the paper –

Proportions and scale also apply in a general way, of course, to the idea or composition and its relative size to your sheet of drawing paper. Initial planning and consideration are important, otherwise you may find to your disappointment that you are well advanced with a drawing which is not going to fit your sheet of paper. In most cases you will be scaling down subject matter to fit your drawing. This involves keeping everything to relative proportions while reducing the overall idea to an acceptable size.

A reliable way to work is to start from the centre of your subject matter, matching this to the centre of your drawing paper. Take one or two general measurements using the pencil or viewfinder technique described earlier in this section (see illustrations **71** and **72**). A couple of freehand diagonal lines will give you the middle of your sheet of paper and you can gradually plan out the main shapes from here. Start with the object nearest the centre of your chosen idea. Once you have estimated the proportions of this in relation to the dimensions of the complete idea you can sketch it in based on similar proportions in relation to the size of your paper. Sketch in the main shapes lightly and roughly at first. If everything seems to fit, go back and check proportions and shapes more carefully. If the size of your preliminary sketch was too big or too small, then obviously you can adjust it accordingly.

Look at the sequence of drawings in illustrations **79–82**. In illustration **79** the building is crammed up into the top right-hand corner – not what I wanted! The next three illustrations show how I should have prevented such an error. I have matched up the scale and position of a 'key' part of the building with the middle of my drawing paper first (illustration **80**). Next I have added the outlines of the main shapes (illustration **81**). Satisfied that these are in the right place, I have developed the drawing in pencil and wash (illustration **82**).

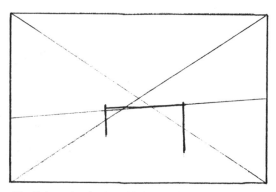

Illustration 79 Bad positioning

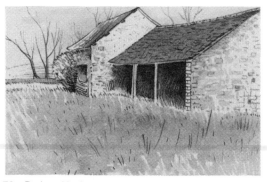

Illustration 80 Using a few basic guide lines to help fix the correct scale and positioning

— **84** —

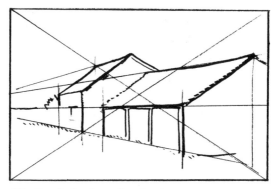

Illustration 81 Developing the outline drawing

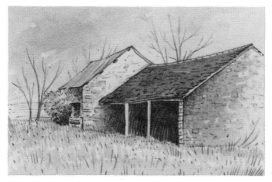

Illustration 82 Final drawing correctly positioned

Projects

1   Take an ordinary breakfast cereal box. Place it on its side or upright but at an angle and about one metre away from you. Make three perspective drawings from different viewpoints, like those shown in illustrations **70a–d**.

2   Get someone to stand in an open doorway so that you can also see into the room beyond. Ignoring the doorframe, make a drawing of the figure and anything seen in the background. Aim for a drawing which gives a good sense of space and depth. Check the proportions of the figure (see illustration **73**) and the scale of the figure to the objects beyond (see illustration **77**).

6
——— USING A ———
SKETCHBOOK

Look upon the sketchbook as your most essential item of equipment and something to use frequently. Ideally, to keep 'in trim' and have plenty of practice, you should draw every day, even if this is only for 10 minutes. Your sketchbook will suit these daily practice sessions just as it will come in handy for research, ideas, thoughts, jottings, experiments, problem solving, notes, planning, roughs and so on. Use it purposefully. Sketching is a means of thinking with your pencil, collecting important information and evolving ideas. You will see from this chapter how valid this aspect of work is, as well as the variety of sketching techniques you can use.

——— Choosing a sketchbook ———

Sketchbooks are sold under a variety of names: sketch blocks, drawing pads, layout pads, and drawing books, for example. To begin with, buy an A4 spiral-bound cartridge paper sketchbook for general use and a small, pocket-size one to jot down those unexpected ideas, notes and flashes of inspiration. Cartridge paper is fine for most media and techniques but, as your work progresses, you may find that you need a certain type and size of sketchbook which better suits a particular medium. For example, if you work mostly in pen and ink you will find that the smooth paper in a

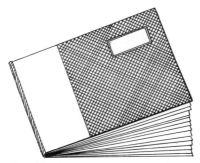

Illustration 83 Sketchbook

layout pad is best; you can also buy sketchbooks consisting of sheets of watercolour paper (for brush and wash ideas), and coloured pastel paper (for chalks, pastels, charcoal and other soft medium techniques). Remember that the type of paper will influence how the medium responds, so think carefully about the kind of sketchbook that will suit you best.

An alternative is to make your own sketchbook using an A4 ring binder and loose sheets. The advantage here is that you can insert sheets of different types of paper and therefore use a whole range of techniques.

——— Ideas and experiments ———

Your sketchbook is your personal visual notebook. You will not have to show it to anyone else and therefore you can work without inhibition. Don't be afraid of making mistakes or 'bad' drawings. This isn't the place for highly finished work. There may be lots of ideas which simply do not work, but this is one of the main purposes of the book – to thrash out ideas and solve problems so that you avoid mistakes elsewhere.

If you are planning a holiday, visiting somewhere, having a day out in the country, or going anywhere that looks potentially promising from a drawing or ideas point of view, then take your sketching things with you. Ideas abound, are often unexpected and come up in the most unlikely places. You need to collect these in your sketchbook so that you have a reserve of starter and outline ideas which you can develop later. For your own interest, make a note of the place and the date, as in the two sketches made with a ball-point pen in illustration **84**.

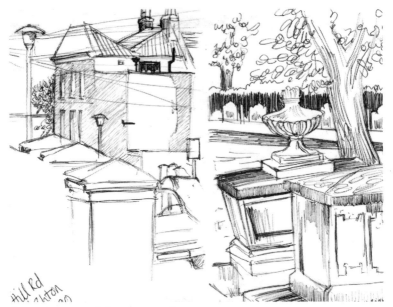

Illustration 84 Collecting ideas. Ball-point pen

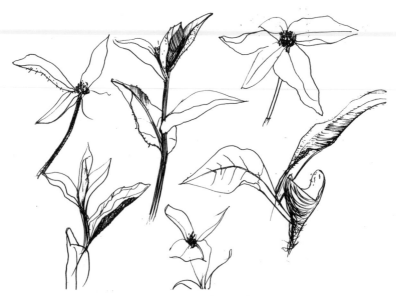

Illustration 85 Preliminary sketches for plant study

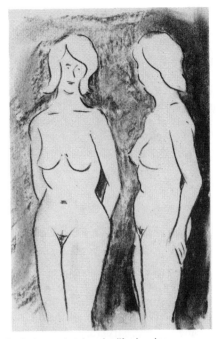

Illustration 86 Preliminary sketches for life drawing

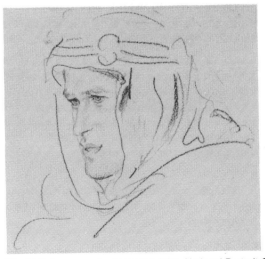

Illustration 87 *T. E. Lawrence* by Augustus John. National Portrait Gallery, London

As well as trying out new media and techniques in your sketchbook, another vital use is for getting the feel of a subject before you attempt a highly-resolved study. Learn to introduce yourself to subjects and ideas in this way, as in the drawings in illustrations **85** and **86**. Quick drawings similar to these will help you assess a subject and its likely problems, getting you looking and thinking. Notice, too, the different techniques used here: a fountain pen in illustration **85** and charcoal in illustration **86**. Experiment with plenty of techniques. Charcoal is an ideal medium for quick results. We have seen the power and potential of line in Chapter 4. Sometimes a sketch works as a very effective drawing in its own right (see illustration **87**).

——— **Drawing and research** ———

Quite often you will need more than the bones of an idea – you need good reference material from which to work. Therefore, your sketchbook can also be used for making careful studies (illustration **88**), researching form and movement (illustration **89**), exploring different viewpoints (illustration **90**), and showing texture, structure, details and colour reference (see page 38). You can work up a final study from a series of drawings like those shown in illustrations **89** and **90**, while some analysis (illustration **88**) will enable you to fully understand the structure and form of something and allow you to complete the main drawing with confidence.

Don't always use pencil in your sketchbooks. Pastel is good for quick colour studies, charcoal excellent for broad tonal work and there is a variety of free-flowing fast-drying pens to choose from for line work. Additionally, you can combine pen and pencil techniques with quick brush and wash effects, either in tone with diluted Indian ink or in colour with watercolour or thinned coloured drawing inks. Water-soluble pencils are ideal for colour sketches which need to incorporate line and solid colour or wash effects.

Much of your sketching will be done out-of-doors – landscapes, buildings, street scenes and harbours, etc. Here is a reminder of what you might need for sketching trips:

- Sketchpad or drawing board and paper.
- Pencils, pens, charcoal, pastels and other colour media such as water-soluble pencils.

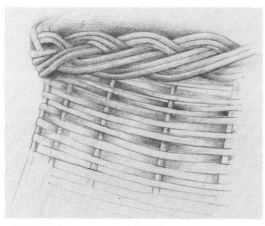

Illustration 88 Analysing structure and detail

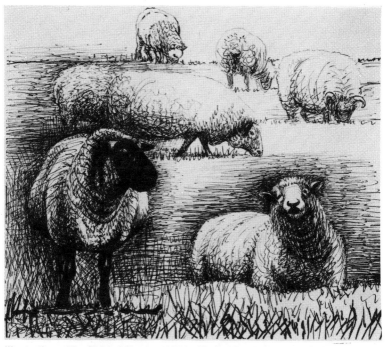

Illustration 89 *Field of Sheep, 1972* by Henry Moore. From the *Sheep Sketchbook*. © Henry Moore Foundation 1993. Reproduced by kind permission of the Henry Moore Foundation

- Small, screwtop bottle of water, brushes, cloth, craft knife, eraser, bulldog clips to hold down paper, fixative.
- Folding stool or something to sit on.
- Rucksack or something to carry everything in.
- Suitable clothing, food and drink.

Be adaptable and prepared for changes in the weather. If you are unable to find or draw exactly what you intended, try something else. If your wonderful landscape view is obliterated by a sudden rainstorm, try some individual studies of clouds or trees from a sheltered spot. And don't expect sheep and other animals to stand still! You may have to work on several sketches at once, like those in illustration **89**.

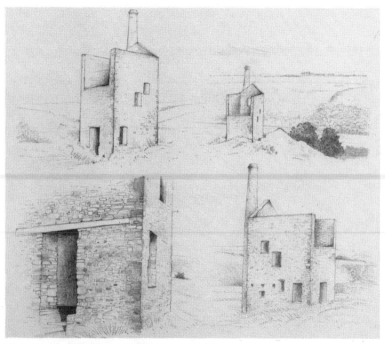

Illustration   90 Exploring different viewpoints

Notes and photographs

You can supplement any sketches, research studies, experiments and details with written notes. Sometimes there just is not enough time to jot

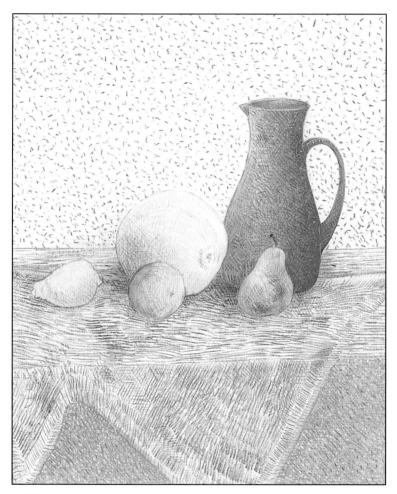

Still life study using line and hatching techniques. Coloured pencils.

Line and wash drawing. The initial drawing was made with a mapping pen and Indian ink with colour subsequently added using weak washes of watercolour.

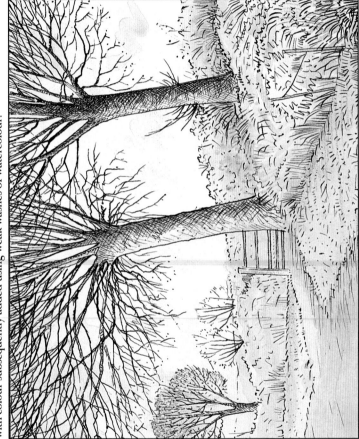

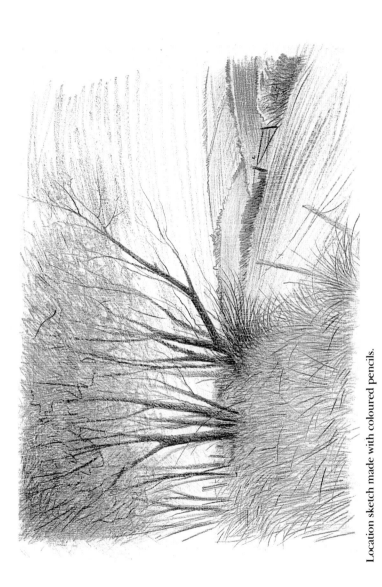

Location sketch made with coloured pencils.

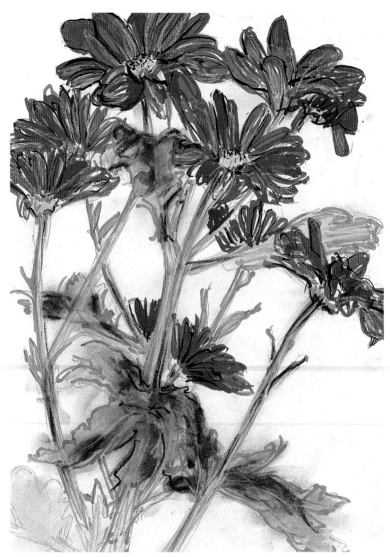
Mixed media drawing using ink, felt pen, pencil and pastels.

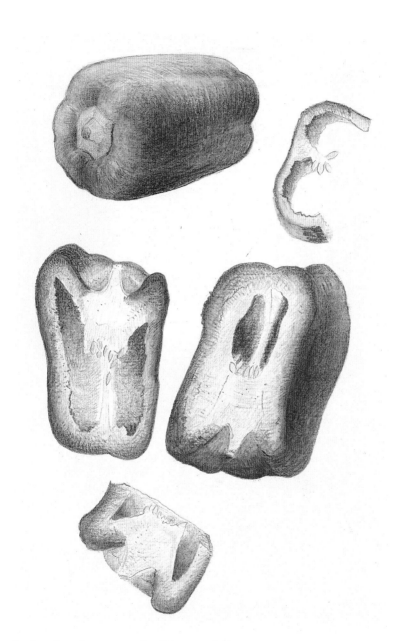

Studies of a red pepper made with water-soluble coloured pencils.

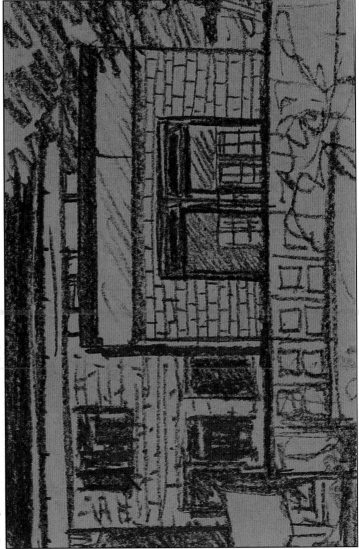

Quick pastel sketch made on coloured paper.

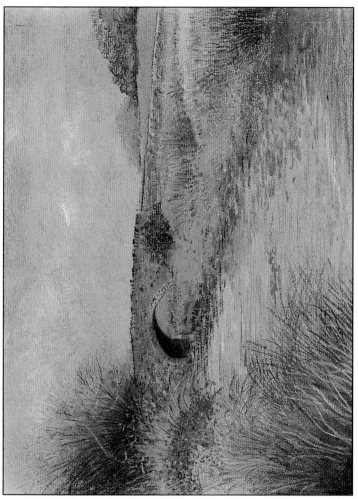
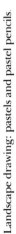

Landscape drawing: pastels and pastel pencils.

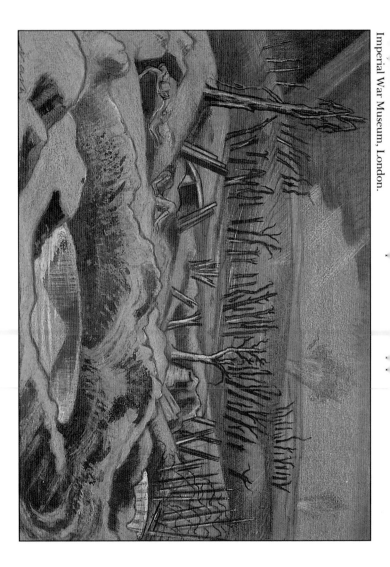

down everything you need to know in the form of drawing and you may, for example, be restricted to black and white when you need some colour reference. If so, do as I have done in illustration **91**, add a few words to your drawing to remind you of things.

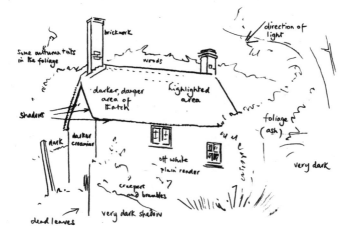

Illustration 91 Annotated sketch

Photographs provide another form of reference. Again, you may run out of time, need something in colour, want a particular detail, or would benefit from a range of viewpoints and different composition suggestions. Look on photographs as an aid to your drawing rather than something to be slavishly copied. In illustrations **92–94**, for example, I can use the photograph to help with colour and detail, while I have made a couple of other sketches which will give me improved ideas for the composition.

Project

Choose an out-of-doors theme which appeals to you. This may be buildings of local interest, tree forms, animals, people shopping, or cloud effects. Over a period of time, make a series of drawings in your sketchbook which will help you compose a well-finished, studio-based drawing later on. Get different views and ideas and use several techniques, including colour.

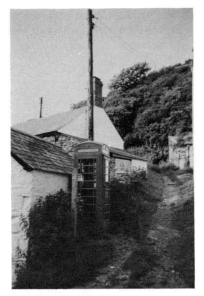

Illustration 92 Location photograph

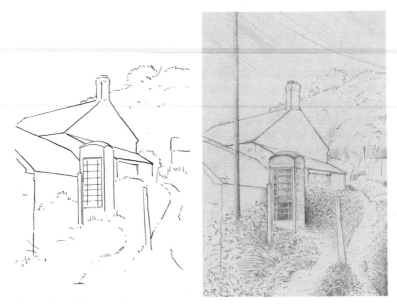

Illustration 93 Location composition rough
Illustration 94 Location sketch

7
—— SELECTING AN ——
INTERESTING IDEA

Handling materials, experimenting with techniques, using perspective, and discovering how to look and see are all essential basic skills when we are learning to draw. And, like other skills, there is always scope for improvement, even for the professional artist. Continually, if slowly, our work should be developing through practice and application, new ideas and techniques, and better ways of expressing ourselves.

The foundation skills acquired in Part 1 can now be put into practice as I encourage you to widen your experiences and tackle a good variety of subjects and ideas. In this part of the book you will see how to make the most of your ideas through selecting and composing, how to plan work thoroughly, and how to develop your ability and find your own means of communicating and expressing using the powerful medium of drawing. As you gain experience you will begin to find a direction in your work, a type of drawing or maybe a specific subject matter that intrigues you most. You can build on this interest and evolve a style of your own – a way of seeing, interpreting and drawing which is stamped with your individual personality.

———————— What to draw ————————

Draw anything and everything! Although you will have your own views about suitable subject matter, avoid getting too narrow-minded and playing safe. You might be moved by the drama of a sweeping landscape or the subtleties of light and dark in a group of objects, the excitement and bustle at a busy railway station or the quiet simplicity of a corner of your garden. The scope is boundless – there are ideas everywhere! Naturally, you will want to choose subjects and themes that excite and interest you. But every drawing needs to be something of a challenge, so avoid repetition. If you have proved that you can draw a particular thing well and have said what you needed to say about it, why draw it again? Repeating something because you know it will work will only lead to tired and uneventful drawings. Look for new viewpoints, new techniques, other ways of doing things. If the drawing demands something new of you, it will not only be more likely to succeed, but also add to your experience and general development. Even if, like Cézanne, you never tire of a few themes, you must be able to view them each time with a fresh eye and keep the drawings vital and lively.

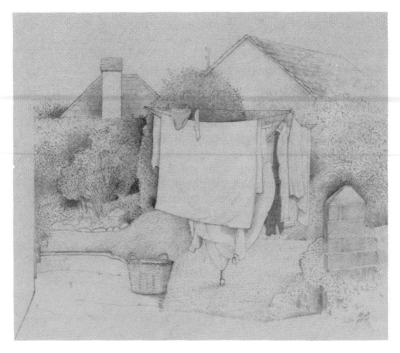

Illustration 95 Ordinary subjects like this can prove surprisingly interesting and challenging. Pencil

You can find ideas and inspiration in the most unlikely places. Look at the range of ideas in illustrations **95** to **99**, for example. I would not expect all of these subjects to appeal to you, but they do hint at the variety of things to draw and the different techniques and media which can be used. In some cases, as in illustration **95**, it could be the relationship of shapes and tones which is the main interest, while in others, such as illustrations **96** and **97**, you can see the potential for using a particular medium or technique. You can get involved with a detailed study of part of a very complex form (illustration **99**), or find that simple, commonplace ones will also inspire lively drawings (illustration **98**).

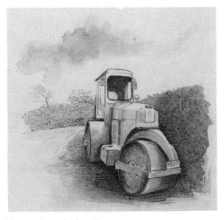

Illustration   96   Line and wash drawing

You are more likely to make good drawings of things you want to draw rather than those you feel you ought to draw. If you have any interests and hobbies it may be possible to develop them further through drawing. A fascination with and knowledge of your subject matter will help you draw it well. So if you are a keen long-distance walker, for example, or a Grand Prix enthusiast, take along your sketchbook and get some ideas to develop.

We have seen that artists draw almost anything and that the classification of subject matter ranges from abstract to detailed realism and embraces ideas developed from fantasy and imagination through to various inter-pretations of natural forms, still lifes, landscapes, figures and portraits. As well as from your own thoughts, ideas, and sketches, you can be inspired by the work, techniques and subject matter of other artists, or find general ideas to develop from photographs and other visual aids.

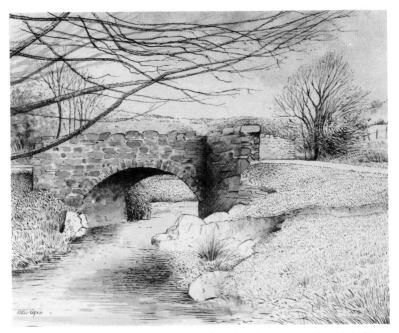

Illustration 97 Mixed media: pencil, brush and wash, pen and ink, and chalks

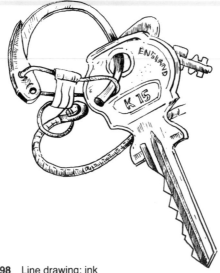

Illustration 98 Line drawing: ink

Additionally, I hope that many of the illustrations in this book will excite you and encourage you to have a go for yourself. Get a taste of the range of subjects, media and techniques by looking at the following illustrations:

- **Natural forms:** illustrations **15, 27–30, 121** and **129.**
- **Still life;** illustrations **33, 35, 39, 44, 55, 63** and **124.**
- **Buildings:** illustrations **3, 10, 12, 49, 56, 64, 77, 82, 90, 101, 130** and **144.**
- **Landscapes:** illustrations **1, 5, 14, 16, 21, 32, 38, 48, 51, 66, 108, 128, 133, 134** and **146.**
- **Animals:** illustrations **50, 89, 115** and **135.**
- **Figures and portraits:** illustrations **6, 11, 31, 86, 87, 127, 131, 145** and **148.**

——— Drawing and design ———

You will remember from Chapter 5 and illustrations **79** and **82** how important it is to plan your drawing so that it fits the paper. However expert you are with materials and techniques and able to express ideas

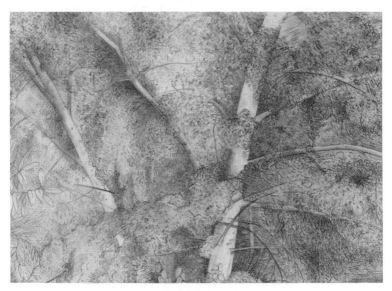

Illustration 99 Detailed study: pencil techniques

well, the impact of a drawing will be drastically reduced if it has been neglected or ill-considered from the design point of view.

But more than just getting the scale right and making sure parts of the idea do not disappear off the edges of the paper, good design will aim to add to the drawing's interest and impact. Indeed, it could well be the key factor in creating an eye-catching and original result. In designing you are composing with different shapes, deciding how best to arrange these in your picture area, what viewpoint or angle to use, how to contrast bold, general areas with smaller, detailed ones and so on. The distribution of tones or colours, the media and techniques to be used, details and textures and what you wish to emphasise and draw attention to are all interrelated to the overall design or composition. Even if you are drawing just a single object you will need to consider its size and position against the background area. So, design relates to the whole sheet of paper and must carefully juxtaposition positive elements (the main shapes and subject matter) as well as negative ones (the background shapes and spaces).

Some of these points are demonstrated by comparing the two drawings in illustrations **100** and **101**. They have the same basic design. In illustra-

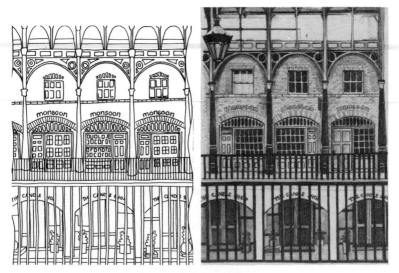

Illustration 100   Line drawing: evenly balanced design
Illustration 101   Pencil study alternative to illustration 100, introducing a more obvious focal point as well as the added interest of tone and texture

tion **100**, in line, the almost evenly distributed weight of the design is more noticeable than in illustration **101**, where the variations of tone and texture disguise it. Notice also that the inclusion of a pendant lamp in the upper left-hand corner has created a more obvious focal point and a shape which can react with the rest, thereby making a more interesting composition.

— How to make a good composition —

Composition involves selecting and arranging in such a way that your eye is led round the drawing, your attention is kept within the picture area, and you focus on a particular point of interest. You will see that good composition can depend just as much on what you decide to leave out as on the way you organise and emphasise the remaining shapes. Again, there is no magic formula for success! As with other aspects of drawing, the wise student will study carefully the theory, advice and various considerations which apply. You must draw with an awareness of these factors rather than a complete conformity to certain rules and procedures. Drawing requires constant thought: with composition you must be fully aware of planning and design and have reasons for your decisions.

One way of helping your own deliberations about composition is to study the work of other artists. Have a look at some drawings by well-known artists – there are some in this book. Look at the way they have composed the work, how they have made the drawing interesting and exciting, whether they have used a focal point or part of the drawing which particularly attracts your interest, and so on. There is more about looking at drawings in Chapter 10. If you can ask and answer the same questions for your own drawings then you will be well on the way to success.

In dividing the picture area up into various shapes and spaces we are again concerned with proportions. Generally speaking, a drawing which uses identical, balanced or totally symmetrical proportions in its basic composition will not have the same overall impact as one which does not. I hasten to add that like any 'rule' in drawing this one is frequently broken with much success by many accomplished artists. However, usually it is best to avoid compositions which use equal splits of the drawing area, either vertically or horizontally. For example, this would apply to a landscape in which the horizon was placed exactly half way up the paper.

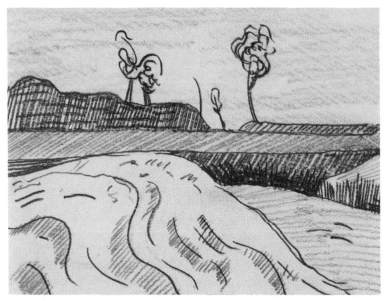

Illustration 102   Composition sketch

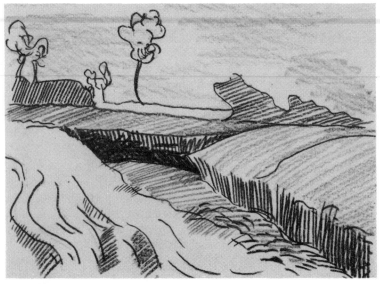

Illustration 103   Composition sketch

Thinking through a composition idea is best done with a series of quick, simple sketches, like those in illustrations **102** and **103**. In the first, the distribution of the main shapes, especially the horizontal lines through the middle and the position of the trees, gives a rather balanced effect. In illustration **103** I have moved the trees and altered the viewpoint somewhat so as to create a more flowing and imbalanced design. Use non-fussy media like charcoal or pastel for roughs of this sort. For easy comparison, they can be done as a sequence on a large sheet of paper, or you can do them in your sketchbook.

Try designs which exploit a diagonal or triangular division or consider the sort of basic split shown in illustration **104**. This uses a proportion known as the 'Golden Mean' or 'Golden Section'. Devised by the great artists and mathematicians of the Renaissance and accepted as having special artistic significance and aesthetic value, it is an arrangement or ratio of proportion such that the smaller part to the larger is the same as the larger to the whole area. Very approximately, the ratio is two:three and this, of course, can be applied in any direction, horizontally or vertically. It means that roughly two-fifths across your drawing you would place some significant feature of the composition. Look back at the position of the trees in illustration **5**, for example, and see if you can identify other drawings which use this principle.

Some other points to watch out for are demonstrated in illustrations **105–107**. In **105** the objects are in a straight row, the gaps between them are similar, the horizon line is straight across, and, with the bottle in the middle, the general arrangement is quite symmetrical. These are all potentially negative points: things which do not contribute to the excitement or interest of the design. In **106** some improvements have been made. The objects are not so spaced out, but although the arrangement is

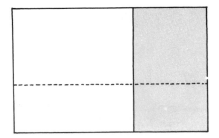

Illustration 104   Using the Golden Section

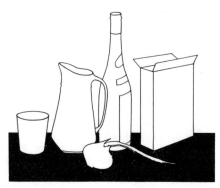

Illustration 105 Composition sketch. Notice that the grouping is rather equally spaced and balanced

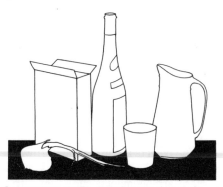

Illustration 106 Composition sketch. Improved grouping with more interesting spaces but still rather symmetrical

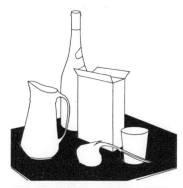

Illustration 107 Composition sketch. Here there is more movement in the design and the grouping is generally more exciting

more interesting the bottle is still very central and the bases of the objects remain level. The composition in illustration **107** I consider to be much better. There is more movement and direction, more interesting spaces, and the general composition is now not so rigid and balanced. These are the sort of points to look at, not only when arranging a still life group, of course, but regarding the selection and composition of any idea.

Summary points

- Use simple roughs and diagrams to plan your composition.
- Consider the size, shape and best way round to use your paper.
- Think about the contrast between sizes, shapes and spaces, as well as movement and direction.
- Avoid basic divisions which will make your composition balanced or symmetrical.
- Use lines and shapes which lead to a main focal point or centre of interest.

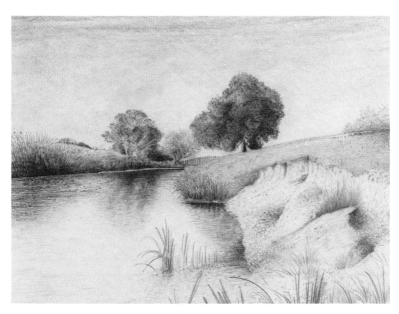

Illustration 108   Selecting from a landscape view

Using a viewfinder

Some subjects are complicated and extensive and therefore it is some-times very difficult to know which part to concentrate on for your drawing. Busy street scenes, panoramic landscapes, and general views fall into this category. A landscape drawing such as illustration **108** has to be selected from many possibilities. The viewpoint and scope of the view are vital considerations in achieving a good composition.

To help you isolate parts of a complex subject in order to determine which area will make the best drawing, you can use a cardboard viewfinder. Make this by cutting an aperture of about 2cm × 3.5cm in the middle of a sheet of 10cm × 13.5cm card. Sizes can vary according to the scale of work. With one eye closed look through the viewfinder and move it around to compare views. See illustration **109**. Try it both landscape (horizontally) and portrait (vertically) ways round.

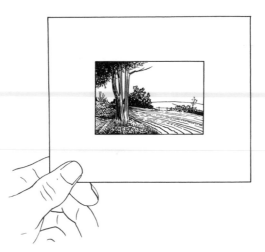

Illustration 109 Using a card viewfinder

Cropping

The composition and occasionally the impact of the drawing can generally be improved by cropping. This means reducing the size of the drawing.

Use two right angles of card like those shown in illustration **110**. These can be moved around on the drawing to 'frame' the best section. The drawing is then trimmed down to the desired size.

This is not a technique for which I would advocate frequent use but it can salvage some drawings which have run into problems with large, uninteresting or repetitive areas, as in illustration **110**. Some unexciting, large drawings can sometimes make two exciting small ones!

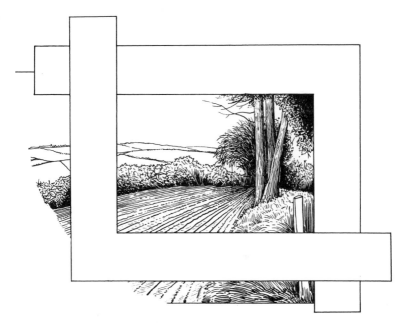

Illustration 110 Cropping

Project

Using a cardboard viewfinder, go round the house and look for interesting corners and subjects to draw. Experiment with different viewpoints and with both 'portrait' and 'landscape' shapes. Make composition roughs of six different ideas. Evaluate the ideas and decide which composition works best. Enlarge it into a fully worked drawing.

8
WORKING THROUGH STAGES

We have seen that drawings are made for many different reasons and consequently can vary from a quick sketch to a highly detailed study. Drawings can be just as powerful and effective as paintings or any other form of expression. As your skills develop and you become more involved in drawing you will recognise this potential and will want to make some drawings which are large and elaborate. These will obviously take a good deal of time, will probably be developed from research and preliminary investigation, and will need sound planning and preparation.

If we redraw something then it may well lose the vitality and spontaneity of the original. Therefore, when planning a drawing, we need to strike a balance between overdoing the preparation such that it stifles the vigour of the drawing, and proceeding with an ill thought out idea which ends in frustration and disappointment. So always leave something to be discovered in the final drawing while having clear aims and intentions and having made justified decisions about scale, composition, techniques, and so on.

Planning your drawing

Look upon planning as a means of enquiry and decision making which will lead you to the best approach to explore in your main drawing. Familiarise yourself with all the points listed below and get used to doing a quick mental check of these prior to each drawing. Not every drawing will need to evolve through all of these stages, of course. But you should be aware of the sort of factors to consider because these influence the way that the work develops. Eventually you will start to follow this process of decision making automatically and more intuitively.

For studio compositions and major drawings you may have to consider all of the following stages of working:

- **Aims**: Your drawing is a visual statement, so what do you want to say? Think carefully about the subject matter and the sort of emphasis and impact you want to achieve. Make some rough plans and ideas.
- **Research**: Get what information you need in the way of sketches and studies. Decide which media and techniques will work best for the effects you want.
- **Composition**: Make some composition roughs to try out alternative ideas before finalising the design.
- **Preparation**: The paper may need stretching or preparing in some other way. Check that you have all the equipment and materials you will need to complete the drawing.

Whatever the subject matter you will find that you work more positively and successfully if you are trying to create something specific and have well-defined aims. If you know what you are trying to achieve in the drawing you are more likely to achieve it! Your aim could be to make a carefully observed and detailed study of something, or be more personal, such as capturing your response to a stormy landscape, or perhaps analytical, for example examining the relationship of shapes and tones in a particular subject. Equally, the aim could be concerned with a special technique or medium. It will set you a problem and focus your attention in a certain direction.

So, you can use roughs to:

- **Get you started** – for thinking on paper, brainstorming and experimenting with basic ideas.
- **Help you understand** – as preliminary sketches to familiarise you with the subject matter before tackling it in detail.
- **Select and compose** – as quick sketches of different parts of a complex subject to help you select an area for closer scrutiny in the main drawing; and as a means of trying out different design and composition alternatives.

- **Try out techniques** – use quick sketches to test out the suitability of a medium for a particular idea or effect, or to check the compatibility of medium and paper or of different combinations of media.

A rough is a simple, small sketch – usually just a few lines made with a pencil or pen (see illustration **93**, for example). You can make the roughs in your sketchbook or as an easy-to-compare sequence on a large sheet

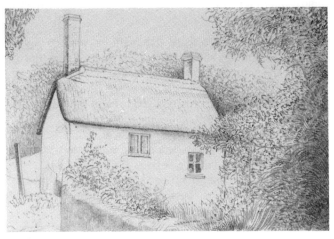

Illustration 111   Research: location drawing

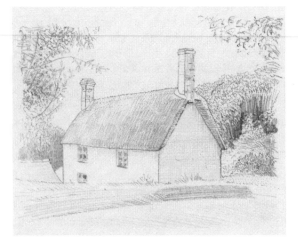

Illustration 112   Research: alternative location sketch

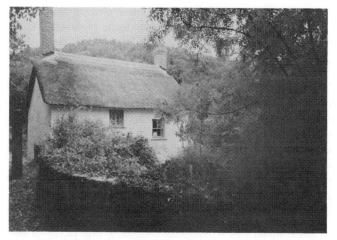

Illustration 113   Research: location photograph

of paper. Try using other quick sketching media, such as pastel, charcoal and felt-pen, as well as pencil.

You will also need your sketchbook for more deliberate studies and investigations in the form of research. Occasionally, you might attempt some themes which are composite in approach, that is made up of a number of different ideas. Other subjects could be moving or changing in some way, or of complex scenes, locations or situations. Time and practical considerations will often prevent the main drawing being made on the spot and the work has therefore to be developed from sketches, studies and other resource material and information. Even when drawing a still life or model in the comfort of your own home, it might still be necessary to leave the main drawing in order to make a separate study of a feature or detail. This will give you a better understanding and help solve problems before tackling this part in the main work. What if you were trying to capture the atmosphere of a bustling crowd at the races, for example, or making a detailed drawing of a church, harbour scene or steam locomotive?

Refer to 'Drawing and research' (see page 90) for some other ideas and information.

Your research can be in the form of:

● **Location drawings**. Use your sketchbook and make some drawings on the spot to give you a general idea as well as specific information about details, textures and features.

- **Preliminary studies**. Investigate different viewpoints, the sort of design and composition you want, and any 'awkward' parts of the subject before you begin the main drawing.
- **Using photographs and books**. This might be essential for imaginative ideas where first hand reference is not possible. Remember that this sort of material is for reference rather than copying.
- **Inspiration from other artists**. Visit galleries and exhibitions to view drawings by well-known artists at first hand. Books and videos will also provide information. Studying the work of other artists is another way of increasing your knowledge and understanding of drawing and helping with your own ideas and technical problems. See also Chapter 10, 'Looking at Drawings.'

Look at illustrations **111–113**. Together these give plenty of information from which to make a final, detailed study. The location drawings give two possible viewpoints as well as the necessary tone and detail reference, while the photograph provides a reminder about the colours.

—— Enlarging and reducing ideas ——

Frequently, the main drawing is worked up from a much smaller composition sketch and it is therefore important to ensure that the larger sheet of paper is in proportion to the smaller. The quickest way of doing this is to place the sketch on the larger sheet of paper so that the bottom edge of the sketch and its left-hand side are aligned exactly with those of the big sheet. If you now place a long straight-edge diagonally across the sketch from bottom left to top right you can extend this diagonal across the larger sheet of paper. Any rectangle constructed with its top right-hand corner on this diagonal will be in proportion to the original sketch. See illustration **114**. You can, of course, scale down ideas by simply reversing the process.

It is not usually necessary to enlarge a rough idea very accurately, although you will want to get the general shapes and proportions approximately correct. The quickest method is to use guidelines drawn diagonally and to divide the paper in half in each direction. Do this with faint lines on both the sketch and the large sheet of drawing paper. You can see where the main lines and shapes of the drawing come in relation

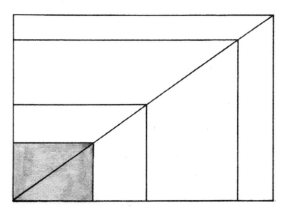

Illustration 114 Enlarging in proportion

to these guidelines and so match them to the corresponding guidelines on the big sheet. If you do not want to damage the sketch, cover it with tracing paper before drawing in the guidelines.

For greater accuracy, use the squaring-up method shown in illustrations **115** and **116**. Draw a grid of squares across the original drawing (or on tracing paper covering it). Measure along each side to work out how many squares to use. Avoid a large number of squares as this can complicate the process. If the drawing does not divide into an exact number of squares, don't worry, as the same will happen to the proportionally larger sheet. Draw a grid on the large sheet which uses a corresponding number of squares in each direction. Look at the original sketch and, taking each square in turn, redraw the part of the drawing in that square on a larger scale to fit the appropriate square on the big sheet. Carry on with this process until you have completed the enlarged outline. You can then erase the unwanted faint grid lines.

Preparing the paper

Some artists like to have the paper loose on the drawing board so that they can twist it round and get at the drawing easily from any angle. Others prefer the paper pinned to the board or held with board clips or bulldog clips. Remember to use paper which is sufficiently large so as to allow for a margin around the edge of your drawing area – this gives scope for mounting the drawing if required for framing or presentation.

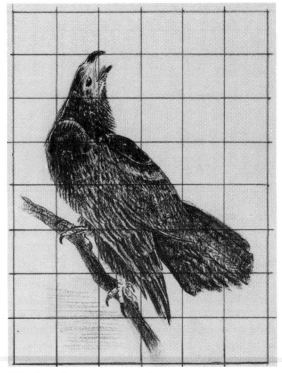

Illustration 115 Squaring-up

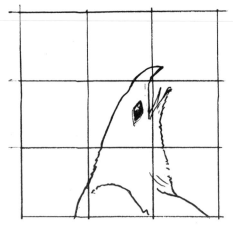

Illustration 116 Enlarging from the squared-up original

Most papers which are going to be wetted in the process of completing the drawing will need stretching. This will stop the paper drying in a cockled or distorted state. The exception is heavy quality watercolour paper.

If all you wish to do is lightly tint the drawing here and there with a little wash then you need only 'dry-stretch' the paper – fix the dry paper to the drawing board with a strip of gummed tape along each edge. For wetter techniques you will need to follow the process shown in illustration **117**. The paper must be of a size which allows a margin of at least 4cm all around on the drawing board. You will need a strip of gummed tape for each side of the paper cut to a length which is slightly longer than the paper. Dip the paper in clean water so that both sides are wetted (illustration **117a**). Position the wet paper on the board (illustration **117b**). Working quickly, apply the wetted gummed strips to each edge. Ensure that the edges of the paper are flat to the board (illustration **117c**). Fold over the overlaps and leave to dry (illustration **117d**). Use a wet sponge to press the tape in place if necessary. If the paper begins to

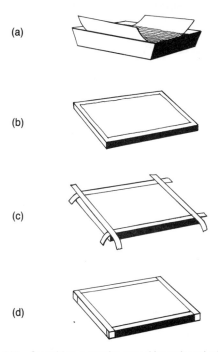

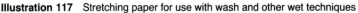

Illustration 117   Stretching paper for use with wash and other wet techniques

wrinkle, let the tape follow the wrinkles – don't force it flat so that it creases. Allow the paper to dry in a flat position at room temperature.

You may want a general background tone or colour for your drawing. This can be done by dry-tinting with pastel or charcoal, working the shaded medium into the surface of the paper with a sponge. Alternatively, you can apply a wash to the whole area using diluted ink or paint applied with a very large brush or a sponge. See illustration **118**.

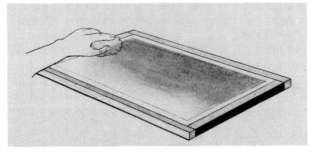

Illustration 118   Dry-tinting paper with a background tone

— Different subjects and projects —

At the start of each major drawing project you will need to make an assessment of your aims for the drawing and how these are going to be realised. You also have to consider how the decisions you make in respect of approach and outcome will affect the techniques and media you use and consequently the paper or support to work on. Some projects may need just a few quick sketches to resolve the idea and composition; others may require extensive research and preparation. Whatever the complexity of the proposed project, some preliminary thoughts and planning are usually a very worthwhile introduction to the idea, will identify any likely problems, and will establish a sense of purpose and the desired objectives.

Now look at illustrations **119–127** to see the sort of evolutionary stages a drawing may go through. Here are three entirely contrasting subjects developed with various media and having different aims. I have illustrated only three main stages for each piece of work: the development is gradual and many others could have been shown. Try some similar subjects for yourself and see how working through stages helps to develop the drawing confidently and successfully.

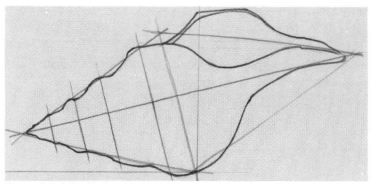

Illustration 119   Shell: constructing the basic outline

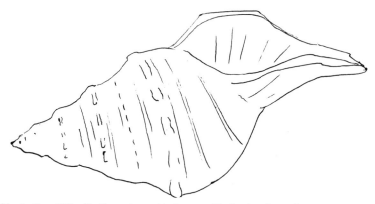

Illustration 120   Shell: erasing guide lines and indicating the main structure

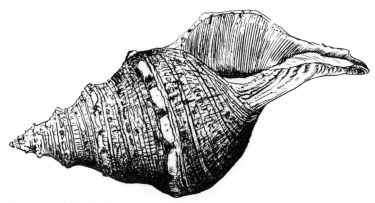

Illustration 121   Shell: developing with tone, texture and detail

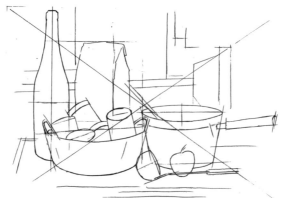

Illustration 122   Still life: basic planning and composition

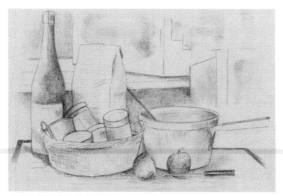

Illustration 123   Still life: indicating general tones

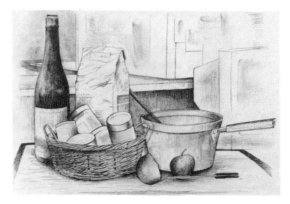

Illustration 124   Still life: adding details

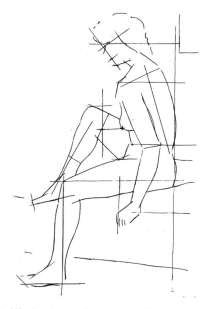

Illustration 125 Life drawing: preliminary sketch

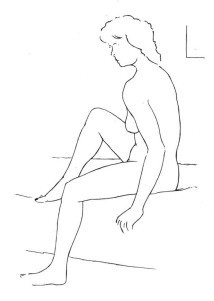

Illustration 126 Life drawing: developing accurate proportions and outlines

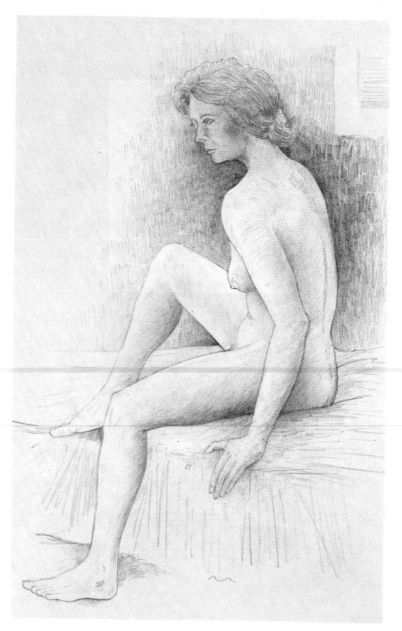

Illustration 127   Life drawing: modelling with tone and adding details

Projects

1 Work on the theme of ruins or derelict buildings. Collect some research material in the form of personally observed drawings (see illustrations **3, 79** and **90**), as well as photographs and other visual reference. Work from these to produce a large, well-resolved drawing on an A2 sheet of paper which uses contrasts of tone or colour to add to the drama and impact of the idea.

2 Try a series of preliminary studies of a cat, dog or other pet. Work from different viewpoints, spending about 10 minutes on each drawing. Get as much information as you can, including colour reference and especially looking at features and particular characteristics. Use these to make one larger, well-finished study in colour.

3 Alternatively, work from a human model, nude or clothed, relating the figure to the background. Follow the same procedure of preliminary sketches worked up into a final drawing in colour.

9
———— DEVELOPING ————
YOUR ABILITY

You will never tire of drawing because there is always something fresh to learn or discover. Now that you have studied all the basics – materials, techniques, and processes (and, I hope, found the time to practise them thoroughly), you will want to try out your own ideas and to start to develop an individual way of drawing.

Getting to the point where you have a recognisable style and you are beginning to succeed in making the sort of drawings which truly reflect your ideas and feelings takes time, of course. To draw well and to make real progress requires much perseverance and practice. Ideally you should be drawing every day, even if this is only a 10 minute sketching session. Drawing is a combination of skill, perception and attitude. As well as the resolve to practise and persevere, you will need the will to experiment and confront new ideas and the determination to tackle problems as they occur.

Whichever direction you take or path you seek to explore, your foundation skills will give you a good starting point. For many artists these skills remain at the focus of their work and, indeed, they are skills which can constantly be improved. With other artists the approach is gradually modified and developed away from formal values and the reliance on objective study and representational outcome. However, basic skills remain important and influential and simply cannot be cast aside at a stroke.

Style is the distinctive or characteristic way of working which identifies a particular artist. Artists like Van Gogh or Picasso, for example, have no need to sign their drawings, for their signatures and personality are embodied within the drawing. Their style is immediately recognisable. In the main, artists do not set out to create a certain style, it evolves over a period of time. Your style will be the result of a combination of factors – the media and techniques you use, your subject matter, and your own personality and how you see and react to things. One of these factors often dominates. An artist's drawings may be instantly recognised because of the specific subject matter, for example, or an unusual technique. So avoid trying forcibly to create a style, let it grow naturally. As you pursue certain subjects, develop particular techniques, and draw with increasing freedom and confidence, so your style will emerge.

Especially for those who are just beginning, drawing needs a breadth of experience, I believe. How else are you going to find out which subjects and techniques excite you the most? Inspiration isn't always a bolt from the blue! You have to try out different ideas and experiences. Sometimes the inspiration is not the initial experience, but develops during the making of the drawing as you see an unusual, clever or alternative way of progressing. Inspiration is easier for the more experienced, for they are

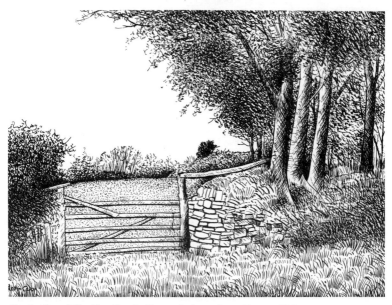

Illustration 128   Creating feeling and atmosphere. Pen and ink

better able to visualise the full potential of an idea, with probably a variety of ways of drawing it. But, whatever you are drawing, try to get fully involved and excited by it. If you are excited, the drawing is likely to show it and, in return, excite others.

Eventually you may want to specialise and concentrate on themes and subjects that especially appeal to you, but this should grow out of a good, general understanding of drawing. You will see from this chapter that drawings can rely on memory and imagination as much as observation and analysis. You may also like to try an approach which selects and organises to create a more abstract outcome.

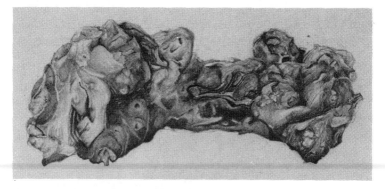

Illustration 129   Relating shapes and tones. Pencil

Drawing and discovering

Even if you have planned your work very carefully, you are never quite sure what is going to happen once the drawing is under way. To an extent, every drawing is a voyage into the unknown, a voyage of discovery, and this is as it should be. What you find out during the drawing process might be something about the subject matter, about the method or medium you are using, or about yourself. And although this discovery may seem very small in itself, each one adds to your wider knowledge and skills.

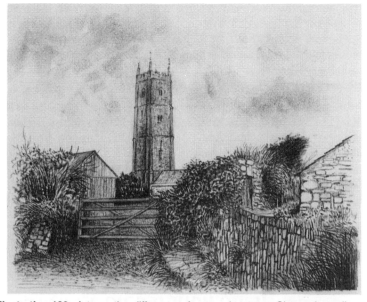

Illustration 130   Interpreting different surfaces and textures. Charcoal pencil

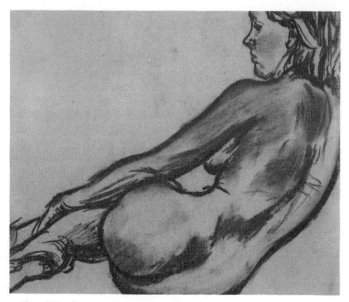

Illustration 131   Form and movement. Charcoal

It follows that the more you draw, the more you will discover; the greater the scope of your subject matter and technique, the greater your drawing experience. So don't be afraid of drawing something. Rather, see what you can find out by drawing it. Sometimes it is a good idea to do this by picking a subject at random. In addition, you can see what you can discover about effects and techniques by trying out a new medium.

Let's look in turn at the variety of drawings in illustrations **128–131**. There is a good range of subject matter but notice also that each drawing uses a different medium. And as well as the experience of various subjects and media, the drawings reveal other factors which add to our understanding and skills: creating feeling and atmosphere (illustration **128**); the relationship of shapes and tones (illustration **129**); interpreting the different surfaces and textures (illustration **130**); and the way we can suggest form and movement (illustration **131**).

——————— Using your memory ———————

Imaginative and fantasy ideas usually rely to some extent on working from memory and it is possible, of course, to make a drawing entirely from memory. Additionally, preliminary sketches and research drawings won't be able to contain every detail of the information you want and therefore you may have to use a certain amount of invention, experience and memorised information to complete the work. And time is often against us when we are out and about sketching, preventing us from completing the drawing, especially if we attempt something quite detailed, as in illustration **132**. The finished drawing (illustration **133**) must, therefore, use a mixture of observed fact, areas developed from notes and other reference material, and what we can remember.

So, as an artist you need to train your memory; you need to have a good visual vocabulary, as it were, which you can refer to when needed. The way to improve your memory is to do plenty of observation drawings of a wide variety of subjects. Fill your sketchbooks with them. This will not only get you into the habit of drawing in such a way that you are looking, examining and understanding, but it will also mean that you are more likely to be able to recall those shapes and draw them from memory if need be.

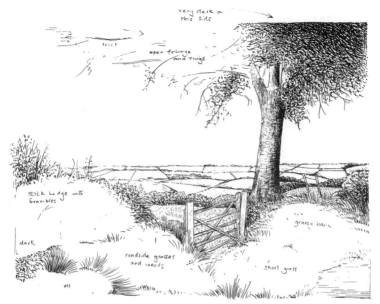

Illustration 132 Unfinished location study with added notes

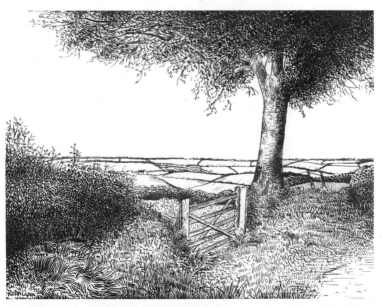

Illustration 133 Landscape drawing worked from a location study, notes and memory

— **127** —

—— Working from visual material ——

You can make drawings from photographs, magazines and newspaper cuttings, and other printed images and illustrations. But beware! There are artists who totally reject the idea of using second-hand imagery as source material. On the other hand, there are those who justify the projection of a transparency on to a sheet of paper so that they can draw round the outlines. There is probably a happy compromise.

Certainly, photographs are a good form of reference and you can work *from* them. We have already seen that they can provide good back-up information to sketches and other research drawings, especially if you want to explore different viewpoints and composition ideas or you want specific detail or colour reference. There are even occasions when the photograph could be copied – as part of a drawing where you need the exact detail, for example. But, on the whole, photographs are aids, starting points, and supplementary reference: they are not for copying.

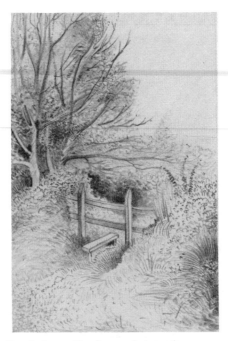

Illustration 134   Developing an idea from a photograph

There are two main reasons why you should not directly copy a photograph. The first is that your drawing needs to be your idea and as lively and spontaneous as possible. This is difficult if you are simply reworking something else. Secondly, photographs often distort distance and perspective and it becomes difficult to translate something like the view down a street, for example, into a convincing drawing. Obviously this may depend on the quality of your camera, but you will notice in many photographs that vertical lines frequently tilt inwards and that the perspective of buildings and similar objects is exaggerated. Equally, depending on the camera and the processing, colours can be approximate to say the least. So try to confine the use of photographs to:

- **Supplementary reference**: as a general reminder of the subject, or to give you a piece of specific information for part of your drawing.
- **Starting points**: as the basis of an idea which you can develop or interpret in a different way.
- **Fleeting moments**: subjects like ripples on the water or a passing express train which you simply would not have time to draw.
- **Composition aids**: to give you different viewpoints and ideas from which to design your drawing.

Where possible, use your own photographs, because if you took them it means that you have at least witnessed the actual scene or subject and

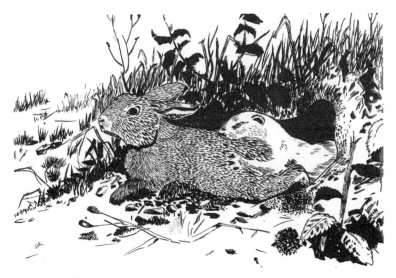

Illustration 135 Working from a photograph. Ink drawing. Student

can, therefore, also work from your impressions and feelings about it. In illustration **134** I have made the drawing from one of my photographs, but have altered the composition somewhat. Because this is a place that I know well, I am able to draw it with some feeling and conviction. You would not be able to draw a subject like the one in illustration **135** from observation, so you have to rely to some extent on photographic material. As here, you have to remember that you are not producing another photograph, but instead have to be sensitive to the drawing process involved. There are many ways photographs can be useful as starting points for studying tone and shape or developing a selective or abstract result, as in illustrations **136** and **137**.

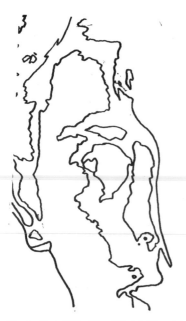
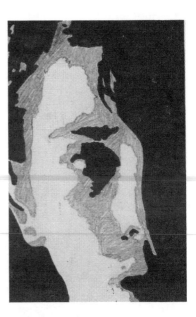

Illustration 136   Simplified outline drawing based on a photograph
Illustration 137   Simplified tonal study based on a photograph

——— Fantasy and imagination ———

In illustration **138** I wanted to express a feeling of fear with some strong imagery and relying on powerful contrasts of tone. In illustration **139** the drawing was made to illustrate a scene from *The Flying Dutchman*. For the first drawing I had no facts to go on at all – it is pure fantasy. For the second, because I was illustrating part of a story, I had some facts as a starting point but had to rely on my imagination to interpret the storyline into a drawing.

Many artists work from imagination rather than observation: they draw from ideas in their head rather than by sitting in front of objects or a scene. Whatever our approach or style, or our philosophy towards drawing, we all need to use imagination in our work to some extent. Now and again it is good for you and your work in general if you freely express yourself in this way.

Inspiration for this sort of work might come from a number of sources: through particular interests, for example science fiction or mythology; from books, poems and films; from travel; by interpreting observed subjects in a much more personal way; from the work of other artists; and by setting yourself a theme to research and develop in an imaginative way. Think best how to use techniques and media to add to the individuality of the work and remember that you may need to exaggerate, distort or use an unusual viewpoint or context in order to create the right feeling and impact in your drawing.

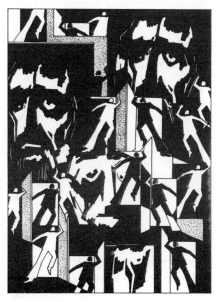

Illustration 138   Fantasy and imagination

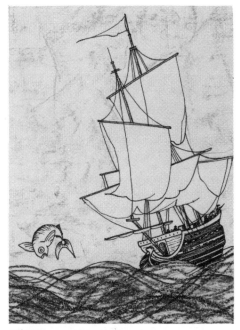

Illustration 139   Working to a theme

———— Abstract drawings ————

It is no doubt easier to see the validity and merit of creating a faithful likeness in a portrait drawing or capturing the atmosphere and feeling of a landscape view than it is to appreciate an abstract result. But not all abstract drawings are just a collection of careless lines and random marks! Your study of drawing should be catholic and wide ranging. Of course, you will want to reject techniques, styles, philosophies and approaches, but this should be done from an informed standpoint rather than one of ignorance.

In fact, many abstract drawings result from applying a particular theory, restriction or emphasis to the drawing process, perhaps to the exclusion of others. You might, for example, be interested in investigating the decorative quality of an idea by reducing it to a series of outlines all drawn with equal emphasis. Alternatively, you could view the subject purely in terms of three tones or colours, and so on. These processes not only

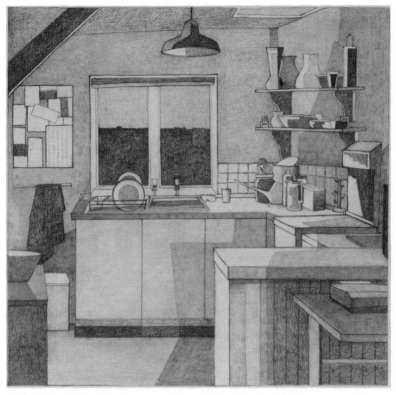

Illustration 140   Achieving a semi-abstract effect by simplifying shapes and tones

produce some exciting results, but are very useful drawing exercises as well.

You can try three main approaches to abstract work: draw from observation but simplify, distort or select from what you see; use lines and geometrical shapes arranged in a deliberate composition and perhaps enhanced with tone or colour; or make random and uninhibited marks to create a free and expressive drawing.

My drawing in illustration **140** was worked from an actual view studied objectively. But, because I have concentrated on a limited range of flat tones related to equally assessed foreground and background shapes, the result is semi-abstract. See also illustration **33**. Contrastingly, illustration **141** is a blot drawing. This is made by drawing on one half of a sheet of paper with ink, then folding it over and pressing it down to offset the

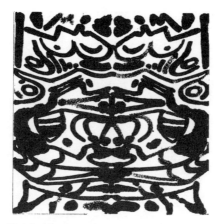

Illustration 141   Blot drawing

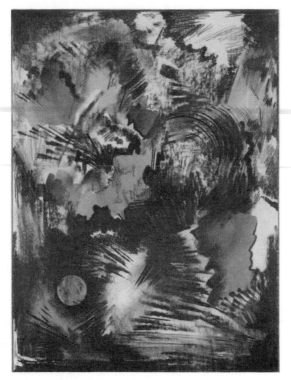

Illustration 142   Mixed media abstract

lines on to the other half. In illustration **142** I have combined various media in a freely expressed drawing, while a collaged technique has been used in illustration **143**. The original line drawing was cut into strips then arranged and glued to a backing sheet. Your abstracts can use an intellectual, ingenious or imaginative approach, can be fun, and at the same time can help you discover much about materials and methods.

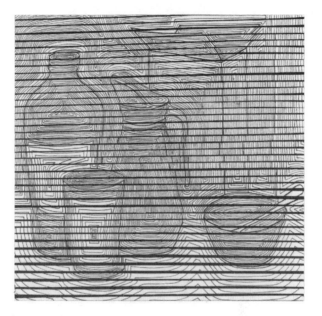

Illustration 143   Collaged abstract

Evaluation

The drawing process is one in which we are constantly making judgements. We are, in effect, being self-critical all the time. We question whether we have made a line too long, whether something is too big, whether we need to make a shadow a little darker, and so on. At the end of each drawing we are likely to spend a few minutes looking at it and assessing its success. Does it fulfil its aims? If it is a preliminary sketch, does it provide enough information to work from? If it is the main drawing, has it got the sort of feeling, effects and impact that you were aiming for?

In addition, we should keep an eye on our general progress and development. A periodic evaluation could take the form of a display of all recent work. By looking at 10 or 20 drawings we can make a better judgement about weaknesses in technique and the sort of things we ought to be practising more, as well as the strengths and interests we should be building on. This kind of assessment helps in making decisions about the future direction of our work and the particular aspects we should be concentrating on.

Constructive self-criticism isn't easy. There is a happy balance between being blasé and expecting everything to righten itself, and being zealously critical to the point of abject depression! Try to justify criticisms and decide on remedies. It could simply be a matter of more practice or revision, or of seeking additional help in the form of books, videos or tuition.

It can also help to get other people's opinion of your work. If you know other artists you could get together for a shared evaluation session. Alternatively, join an art society or club, or enrol on a life class or other drawing course. Here will be an opportunity to meet other artists, both amateur and professional, and to exchange views and ideas.

Projects

1   Develop two drawings, on A2 sheets of paper or larger, on the theme of 'Light and Dark'. In the first drawing work as much as possible from imagination and aim to express the theme in a very individual and personal way. For the second drawing work from a still life group (for example, illustrations **33** and **140**). Make tone (and/or colour) the prime interest in your drawing. For both drawings consider the best media to use and whether your idea would be more effective in colour or on coloured paper.
2   Make an evaluation of your last 10 drawings. In your notebook or sketchbook, jot down any obvious weaknesses and suggested remedies.

10
——— LOOKING AT ———
DRAWINGS

The experience of evaluating your own drawings will help you make informed judgements about other people's. Looking at other drawings is a vital part of the breadth of approach that I recommend. You can enjoy looking at the work of different artists, be excited, interested and stimulated by it, and often learn a great deal about selecting ideas, using techniques and presenting drawings to the best advantage.

Looking at drawings is, therefore, a good habit to develop. Look at everything – work by your friends as well as the drawings of the great masters. Visit exhibitions, galleries and museums. Many provincial museums are surprisingly well endowed with drawings, though they may not all be on show. Go to local exhibitions as well as to see the collections at the British Museum, Courtauld Institute, Ashmolean and other major galleries. Start your own collection of postcards, reproductions, cuttings and books.

——— Historical context ———

Throughout history artists have used whatever tools and techniques were available to express their observations, thoughts, emotions and anxieties in the form of drawings. Cave drawings date back to earliest man, some 40,000 years ago. Many early drawings were decorative, scratched on to pottery, walls or columns, for example, or engraved into metal or carved from wood. Few examples of drawings on paper or parchment exist before the sixteenth century.

The 'modern' age of drawing began with the invention of printing and the woodcut. Artists like Dürer could reach a much wider audience through their illustrations in books and as separate reproductions. But it was in the great Renaissance period of the fifteenth and sixteenth centuries that drawing was seen as an art form in its own right and as the basis for all art. Uccello, Leonardo da Vinci, Michelangelo, Raphael and Holbein were among many notable artists of that time who sought to perfect devices such as perspective, find means of achieving correct proportions, and explore techniques like silverpoint, chalk and charcoal drawing.

As with many forms of art, the history of drawing reflects the outlook and wealth of different ages. There are periods when portrait drawings were fashionable and others when artists were more concerned with nature, religion or the mysteries of the universe. There were times of reaction and invention as well as of celebration and consolidation. The history of drawing is obviously a very extensive subject. If you come across well-known artists whose drawings you find interesting and inspiring then do a little detective work of your own. See what more you can find out about their life and work. Study their subjects and techniques; maybe they will influence your own drawings. Clearly some artists will appeal to you more than others, but find time to borrow books from your local library and begin to develop an appreciation of different artists and styles.

There are some master drawings in this section and also in illustrations **1**, **6**, **11**, **64**, **87** and **89**. These have been chosen to demonstrate different media, techniques and approaches and, above all, variety. They are not all highly finished drawings, of course. Study them to see what you like or dislike about them, and whether they can provide any indicators for your drawings. A comprehensive list of other famous artists to look at would be extremely lengthy, but I recommend the following for consideration: Poussin, Claude Lorrain, Rubens, Rembrandt, Watteau, Gainsborough, Goya, Daumier, Degas, Cézanne, Gaugin, Toulouse-Lautrec, Matisse, Picasso, Klee and Hockney.

—————— Looking and learning ——————

Let's look carefully at the drawing by Canaletto in illustration 144. Venice is a city with elegance, history and atmosphere which has attracted artists for many centuries. This view from a corner of the Doge's Palace looking into St. Mark's Square is a favourite one with

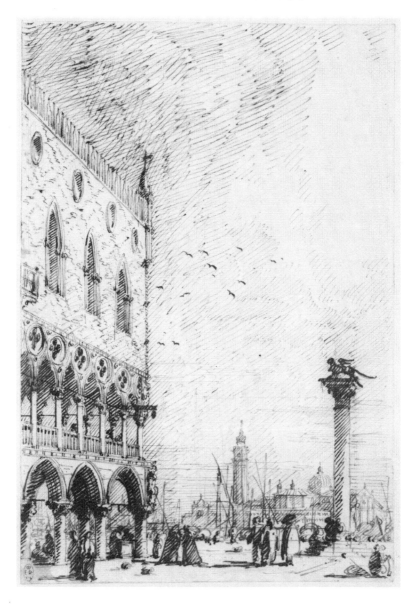

Illustration 144 *Doge's Palace overlooking S. Giorgio Maggiore* by Antonio Canaletto. Pen and brown ink on toned paper. Windsor Castle, Royal Library, © Her Majesty the Queen

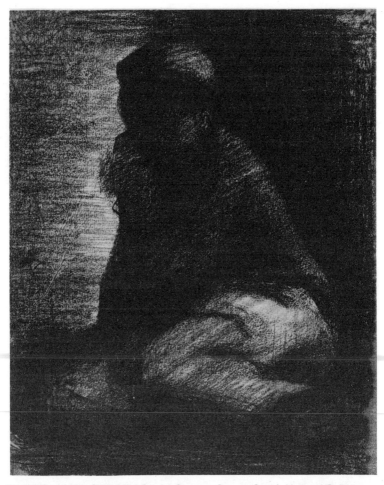

Illustration 145 *Crouching Boy* by Georges Seurat. Conté. National Gallery, London

artists. Is it a good drawing? If so, why is it, and what can we learn from it?

I stressed in an earlier chapter the influence of such fundamentals as size, technique and the type of paper in determining the outcome and impact of the drawing. Reproductions in books are seldom of the same size and

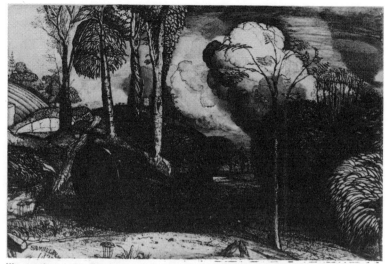

Illustration 146 *The Valley with a Bright Cloud* by Samuel Palmer. Pen and sepia wash. Ashmolean Museum. © University of Oxford

quality as the original, of course. The Canaletto drawing is 27 × 19cm and made in pen and brown ink on a toned paper.

Although like many of Canaletto's drawings this view was probably completed with the help of a camera obscura (a device used to ensure accurate outlines and perspective), the drawing has a feeling for space and atmosphere. It is a sensitive drawing with wonderfully deft pen touches, especially in the arcading of the palace. Notice how lines, birds and pen strokes create a sense of movement and vigour. Shadows and contrasts of tone and scale give a remarkable feeling of depth within a very confined area.

The majesty and scale of the buildings are enhanced by the carefully grouped figures which additionally, with their shadows, give interest to the foreground. A close look at these figures shows that they are suggested with just a few pen lines, rather than being worked in great detail. So, too, with some of the shadow effects – look at the hatched lines on the column and under some of the arches. Our attention is maintained within the picture area, we are led to a distant focal point, and there is plenty to interest us both in subject matter and technique. So, the drawing works: it is a good drawing.

These are just a few points about the Canaletto drawing. They illustrate

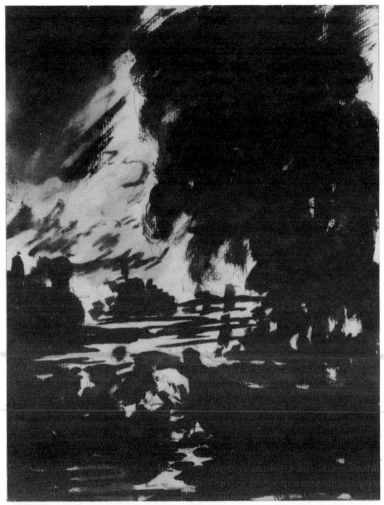

Illustration 147 *Trees and a stretch of water on the Stour* by John Constable. Pencil and sepia wash. By courtesy of the Board of Trustees of the Victoria and Albert Museum

the sort of things we can look for in a drawing and show how by looking, analysing and trying to understand we can develop a greater appreciation of drawings and pick up tips and ideas for our own work.

Something else we should bear in mind as we look at a drawing is the artist's aim or intention. While the Canaletto drawing is a carefully observed study, Constable's *Trees on the Stour* (illustration **147**) is just a quick preliminary sketch and Palmer's *The Valley with a Bright Cloud* (illustration **146**) is more of a visionary landscape than a real one. These artists have different aims, just as they use different media and tech-

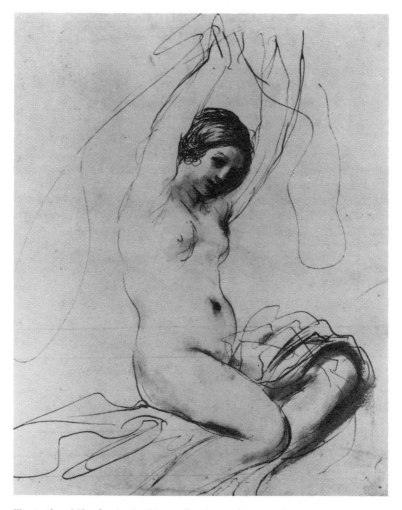

Illustration 148   *Study of a Woman Bathing* by Giovanni Guercino. Pen and wash. © British Museum

niques; similarly, the two contrasting figure drawings in illustrations **145** and **148**. So, although our judgement is naturally influenced by our own preferences, it is more constructive to view a drawing on its individual merits rather than make what are often fairly tenuous comparisons.

Inspiration and ideas

Look at the pose in illustration **148**, the technique in illustration **147**, and the mix of fact and imagination in illustration **146**. As we view other drawings, there are sometimes aspects which spark off ideas for exploration in our own work. Looking at other artists' drawings helps us to form opinions and shape our own philosophy and outlook. Equally, they can be inspirational, clarifying a problem that we have been struggling with for some while, or providing us with a fresh way forward.

While there are benefits from studying other drawings, I should not want to give the impression that we should always look at drawings simply to see how they can help us. Drawings are for enjoyment as well, and remember, to fully appreciate a good drawing you may need to look at it many times.

Project

Study carefully the five drawings in this chapter. Which one gives you the most pleasure or the most inspiration? Make a drawing of your own, inspired by any of the illustrations in this book.

11

── HOW TO MOUNT ── AND FRAME YOUR DRAWINGS

In general you will be producing working drawings and development sketches, rather than exhibition pieces. However, as your work improves and you make some drawings which are particularly successful, you will want to mount and frame a few. You may like to display them in your home or even exhibit some. Drawing is, after all, a means of communicating ideas to other people – so your work should be seen.

── Preparing the drawing ──

Take the drawing you have chosen to frame and check it over to see if there are any final details or alterations you would like to make. Clean off unwanted marks and if necessary spray the drawing with fixative. This will protect soft, smudgy techniques, such as charcoal and pastel, and prevent them offsetting and spoiling. Spray the drawing in a well-ventilated room from a distance of about 30cm. Start at the top and work across and downwards. Spray lightly and allow the work to dry. Test a corner to see if a further coating of fixative is required. Trim the drawing to a size that leaves at least a 2.5cm margin as overlap for the mount.

The way that a drawing is presented is a matter of personal preference: some people like the drawing to hang naturally and are not bothered by any slight surface undulations, while others prefer it to be absolutely flat. Drawings on thin paper may need backing before fixing them to a mount. This is done by gluing the drawing to a sheet of thicker paper or card. Choose a card with a low pH value, preferably acid-neutral, like the Fome-Cor board available from Daler-Rowney. Use a wheat starch powder or water-soluble PVA adhesive, both of which have a neutral pH value. Cut the card to the frame size, outline the position of the drawing, apply a thin, even coating of adhesive to the card and carefully lower the drawing into place. Working quickly and from the centre, smooth out the work towards the edges by pressing down on offcuts of clean paper. Leave the drawing to dry under pressure – the weight of several drawing boards is ideal.

Choosing mounts

Mounts and frames serve both a practical and an aesthetic purpose. Drawings need the protection of glass and, in addition, the mount and moulding should help focus attention on the drawing and enhance its presentation. Therefore, in your decisions about framing a work you need to consider the complete combination of drawing, mount and frame. You may mount and frame some drawings yourself and have others done professionally. Whatever you decide it is a good idea to get some offcuts of mounting card and make right-angle shapes, like those shown in illustration 110, so that you can try out various colours and types of card. Place them round your drawing to see which looks best. Also, if you can beg or buy a few scrap lengths of different framing mouldings from your local picture framer, you can use these in conjunction with the sample mounts to get a fairly accurate impression of the combined effect of mount and frame. As in illustration 149, you might like to choose oval or double mounts, as well as consider the texture and colour of the card.

The mount is usually cut so that it has a slightly wider margin at the bottom than at the sides or top (see illustration 150). The width of these margins will depend on the content and impact of the drawing. However, in general, an A3 drawing will need margins of about 6.5cm, with 7.5cm at the bottom.

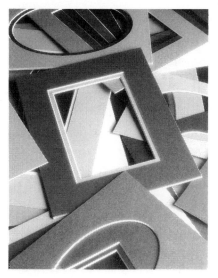

Illustration 149 Various mounts

You can cut a simple window mount with a sharp craft knife used with a metal straightedge (illustration **151**). First cut the card to suit the dimensions of the frame. You can mark off the margins on the back and then cut out the centre piece or, as I prefer, work from the front. Mounts depend on accurate measuring, clean, straight lines, and precise right-

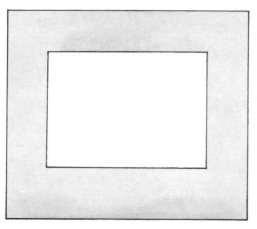

Illustration 150 Cut the mount so that it has a slightly wider margin at the bottom than at the sides and top

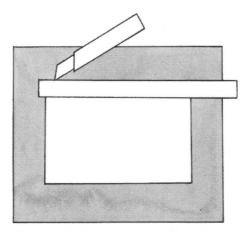

Illustration 151 Cutting a simple window mount with a craft knife

angles. Badly made, they will only detract from the drawing rather than enhance it. As you handle and measure the card, be careful not to mark or damage it in any way. I find that cutting from the front of the mount gives a neater finish. I mark off the width of the side margins with faint pencil lines along the top and bottom edges, then I place a perspex rule across the card and mark the actual corners of the central aperture with a pin. I cut out the centre shape using a very sharp knife against a metal rule, working on a cutting board.

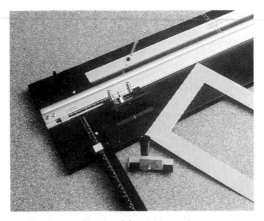

Illustration 152 The Logan Simplex SG700 Mount Cutter available from Daler-Rowney

If you decide to make most of your own mounts you need to invest in a good quality mount cutter in order to get professional results (see illustration **152**). These are available from artists' materials shops: ask for a demonstration. Practise on some old card offcuts first.

Work can also be flat-mounted, that is simply trimmed to the exact dimensions of the drawing and glued to a backing sheet, or you can use a double mount, as in illustration **153**. Fix the drawing to the mount with double-sided framer's tape or by using the hinged method shown in illustration **154**.

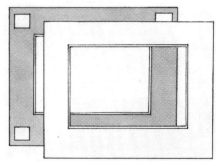

Illustration 153   Making a double mount

There is a huge variety of mounting cards and boards to choose from. However, many of these are not acid-free and consequently may cause some discolouration to the edges of the mounted work over a period of time. There are also problems with the light-fast quality of some cards. Ideally you should use a good quality neutral pH board, such as Daler Studland Board. Similarly, where work is taped to the back of a mount, an acid-free framing tape should be used.

If you lack the time, confidence or equipment to have a go yourself, then discuss any ideas for mounting and framing your drawings with a professional framer.

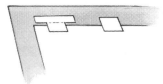

Illustration 154   Fixing the drawing to the mount with paper hinges. Glue one half of the hinge to the back of the drawing and secure the other half to the back of the mount using a cross piece of framer's tape

Choosing frames

Like mounts, frames need to be of a high quality if they are to comple-
ment the drawing to the best effect. You may be interested in buying all
the necessary equipment and making your own frames. Alternatively,
you can have frames made to suit your specifications at a framer's or craft
shop; you can renovate old frames bought from junk shops and market
stalls; you can use frame kits or clip frames; or you can buy cheap framed
prints, replacing the print with your mounted drawing. Illustration **155**
shows how the mount and drawing are assembled within the frame. You
can also order frames by post. Send for samples and details to check the
quality and suitability before placing an order.

The choice of frame moulding should obviously relate to the size and type
of drawing, as well as the mount. Small drawings often look best with a
plain, narrow moulding in natural wood, while larger works can take
something proportionally wider. You might decide to use a coloured
moulding for an abstract, whereas a detailed still life would look better in a
more ornate frame. Have a look round some galleries and exhibitions to
see how other artists have framed their drawings. This will give you
some ideas for your own work.

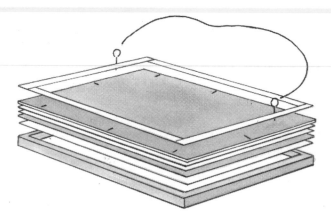

Illustration 155   Assembling the mount and drawing in the frame

APPENDIX 1

Further reading

The following is a list of some recently published books which cover specific topics in more detail:

Complete Guide to Painting and Drawing Techniques and Materials, The, Colin Hayes (Phaidon)

Creative Painting with Pastel, Carole Katchen (Harper Collins)

Drawing: Seeing and Observation, Ian Simpson (A & C Black)

Drawing the Human Head, Louise Gordon (Batsford)

Drawing with Colour, Judy Martin (Studio Vista)

Drawing Workshop, Doreen Roberts (Harper Collins)

Encyclopedia of Coloured Pencil Techniques, The, Judy Martin (Headline)

Encyclopedia of Drawing Techniques, Ian Simpson (Headline)

Figure Drawing and Anatomy for the Artist, John Raynes (Hamlyn)

Figure in Action: Anatomy for Artists, The, Louise Gordon (Batsford)

How to Draw and Paint What You See, Ray Smith (Dorling Kindersley)

How to Draw with Charcoal, Sanguine and Chalk, José M Parramón (Watson Guptill)

Learn to Draw (a series of books on various subjects published by Harper Collins)

Learn to Frame, Sheila Fairbrass (Harper Collins)

Life Drawing in Charcoal, Douglas Graves (Watson Guptill)

Oil Pastel, Kenneth Leslie (Watson Guptill)

Pastel Book, The, Bill Greevy (Watson Guptill)

Picture Framer's Handbook, The, Michael Woods (Batsford)

Sketching, Judy Martin (Harper Collins)

Sketching at Home, John Hamilton (Blandford)

Instructional magazines

Artist, The: 63–65 High Street, Tenterden, Kent TN30 6BD

Artist's and Illustrator's Magazine, The: 4 Branden Road, London N7 9TP

Leisure Painter: 63–65 High Street, Tenterden, Kent TN30 6BD

Home study courses

The Art School, Freepost B, London E18 1BR

Cheltenham Tutorial College, Freepost (GL 1141), Cheltenham GL53 7BR

National Extension College, 18 Brooklands Avenue, Cambridge CB2 2HN

The Open College of the Arts, Houndhill, Worsborough, Barnsley S70 6TU

APPENDIX 2

Glossary of drawing terms

Aerial perspective. The influence of the atmosphere on a distant view so that objects are less distinct, tonal contrasts muted, and colours weaker and cooler. Colours often seem to acquire a bluish tinge as they recede.

Airbrush. A mechanical tool for creating finely controlled spray effects. Compressed air from a canister or compressor is mixed with the paint and directed through an adjustable nozzle to make the spray.

Asymmetrical. A design or shape which, when divided along its central axis (more or less in half), is not identically balanced.

Bleed. The blurring of the edges of a line or shaded area caused when two wet areas meet, a wet wash undercuts a dry charcoal or pastel area, or a wet medium is applied over a dry one. This can also happen when ink or brush lines are applied to the wrong sort of paper.

Blending. The working together of adjacent areas of soft tone to create a gradual transition from light to dark.

Cartoon. A full-size design, often in chalk or charcoal. Usually this is transferred on to a canvas to give the outline for a painting.

Centre of vision. The point on the horizon or at eye-level which is immediately in front of you. This need not be in the middle of the drawing because your viewpoint could be from one side.

Chiaroscuro. Dramatic contrasts of light and dark, as for example in the drawings of Leonardo da Vinci and Rembrandt.

Cockling (Buckling). Uneven paper surface after applications of wash or spray.

Composition. The way you arrange the various shapes and content of your drawing into a particular design.

Draughtsmanship. Skill in drawing.

Elements of drawing. Line, point, tone, texture, colour, form, size, shape and pattern.

Eye-level. An actual or imagined horizontal line in a drawing which represents your line of vision in relation to the subject and shows the position from which your viewpoint is taken.

Figure drawing. A drawing of a human figure.

Fixative. A kind of very thin varnish which is sprayed over soft pencil, charcoal and pastel drawings to prevent them smudging.

Focal point. The object or part of the drawing that most attracts your attention. Usually the design or composition is so devised that shapes and lines lead your eye to a particular point.

Foreshortening. The influence of perspective on an object coming directly towards you, such as an outstretched arm. This gives a very obvious contrast in scale between the nearest part and that furthest away.

Form. The three-dimensional shape of something.

Foxing. Brown spots on a drawing caused by exposure to dampness.

Golden Section. The use of a mathematical proportion of approximately 5:8 in the composition of a drawing. Therefore, the focal point or most obvious feature would come on a line roughly five thirteenths of the way across.

Gradation. The gradual evolution from light to dark shading without any noticeable edges.

Grid. Division of the drawing into squares to help with the organisation of the composition and scale, or for enlarging.

Hatching. Short, closely spaced straight lines used to suggest shadows or texture. The lines are usually slanting and the closer they are together, the more intense is the shading effect. In **cross-hatching**, a series of lines drawn in one direction is overworked with others in the opposite direction.

Highlight. The very lightest area in a drawing. A part that attracts or reflects the greatest amount of light.

Horizon line. A horizontal line, drawn or imagined, which represents your eye-level and the furthest point of sight on the ground area.

Landscape. As well as drawings of the open countryside, this relates to the general shape of a drawing in which the horizontal measurement is significantly greater than the vertical one.

Lay figure. A jointed, wooden model used to help with human proportions and poses.

Light-box. A device used for making tracings. It consists of a box with a clear perspex lid, this lit from inside.

Medium. Any drawing material, such as pencil, charcoal, pastel, and ink.

Mixed media. Using several different drawing tools or materials within the same drawing.

Monochrome. A drawing in black and white or confined to a range of tones of one colour.

Monotone. Using a single tone (shade), plus areas of white; normally black and white.

Natural forms. Shells, bark, plants and other objects found in nature.

Objective drawing. Trying to show the real likeness of something.

Overworking. Adding more work, perhaps in a different medium or technique, over lines and tones already completed.

Perspective. A technique for creating the illusion of distance and space.

Portrait. A drawing of someone's head and shoulders. This term is also used to describe the shape of a drawing in which the vertical dimension is greater than the horizontal one.

Proportion. The size of one object in relation to others. Also, the size of one part of an object in relation to other parts and the object as a whole.

Register. Keeping one sheet of paper exactly in the right position in relation to a sheet beneath, when making monoprints, tracings and copies.

Representational drawing. A drawing which shows something exactly as you see it.

Rough. A quick preliminary sketch to try out an idea.

Sfumato. The careful blending of delicate areas of shading so that there is no obvious distinction between one tone and the next.

Sgraffito. Drawings made by scratching through one layer of colour or tone to reveal a contrasting one beneath. For example, you can scratch lines in to black ink which has been applied over coloured wax crayon.

Shading. Creating light and dark areas in a drawing to give the effect of shadows and the illusion of three-dimensional form.

Stippling. Creating tone or mixed colour by holding a brush, pencil or pen vertically and stabbing it up and down to produce an area of fine dots.

Stretching paper. Preparing paper so that subsequent washes of ink or paint do not distort its surface. See page 115.

Support. Anything used to draw on, like paper and card.

Symmetrical. A completely balanced composition or shape. If divided in half, each half would exactly correspond.

Technique. The process of working in a particular drawing medium or the individual method of using that medium, such as hatching, stippling or linear.

Template. A shape cut from thin card which can be used to draw round in order to repeat the outline several times.

Thumbnail sketch. A very small sketch just to show the simple outlines of an idea.

Tint. Weak colour, usually a thin colour wash added to a drawing.

Tone. The relative lightness or darkness of a colour or the progression from black through various greys to white.

Vanishing point. Lines used in perspective will appear to converge to a point on the horizon or eye-level, known as the vanishing point.

Check the Index for other references to terms and techniques.

INDEX

Numerals in italics refer to illustration numbers